人起活
让想生
总

印象厦门

xiamen
It's evocative of
a good life

厦门大学出版社
XIAMEN UNIVERSITY PRESS
国家一级出版社
全国百佳图书出版单位

金鸡百花　　　红砖古厝　白鹭洲
鹭女神　歌仔戏
　　万国建筑 骑楼　嘉庚建筑　园博苑
江两岸
植物园　经济特区 凤凰花　　工夫茶

植物园

茶面	自贸区	土笋冻		日光岩	鼓浪屿		龙舟赛
南普陀寺	中山公园				嘉庚建筑
妈祖女神	面线糊			南音	环岛路
					白鹭女神

厦门印象
Impression of Xiamen

前言

下门，厦门。

这里是当代中华文明改革开放迎揽八面来风的大厦之门，这里是当年华夏儿女筚路蓝缕、自强不息走下海洋之门。

当清澈长流的九龙江水平缓地淌过海门岛，沿着嵩屿半岛拐了个弯，眼前就是烟波浩瀚的大海了。向东眺望，晨光熹微之中，一列绿如翡翠的岛屿浮现在万顷碧波的那一端，像一道门槛分隔了大江与巨海的浪线。

"下门！下门！"朝霞映得碧海流金。越过鼓浪屿那片被誉为"金带水"的水域，迈出最后一道"门"，就是出海口了。这里连通台湾海峡，连向太平洋……

时空突然纠结成团，细密而奇妙的传说与现实如风般拂面掠过，飒飒有声。想象着当年风雨兼程的先民看到这片通向南洋的海湾时那份激动的情景，或许大海上点点翔舞的鸥鹭依然记得那期盼民族复兴的声声深情呼唤。

厦门名字的传说，归结的还是一个"门"字。打开这扇门，外通九夷八蛮，风潮之所出入，商舶之所往来，至今令人叹为观止；打开这扇门，内接漳泉大陆广袤内地，为渡口之要道，为海洋之要冲，始自凸显地理方位。

开启扣合，不舍昼夜。厦门，地处滨海扼要，立足于内陆与南洋两个扇形面交汇的一道门。它既是中原文化走下海洋的源头，又是闽南文化沉淀流变的源泉，积聚了中西文化的冲击、碰撞、融合，镌刻了河洛民俗的承袭、演变、传播。多源复合的人文社会，使厦门成了兼容并蓄的城市，催发新生事物的摇篮，最终成了闽南文化标新立异的高地。

拥有"海洋性格"的厦门始终坚信，出了海每个方向都是路。这座岛城凭着大海赋予的宽广气势、不息精神和开拓意志，不停地打开一扇扇门——实施城市主体功能扩展，跨出本岛，跨入周边城市，跨过台湾海峡，走向了大洋，飞向了世界，连接了全球。

这座胸中藏海的英雄城市，在中华民族伟大复兴的历史征程中，以大气磅礴之势，一次次让荣耀的坐标注在这片生机勃发的热土上；这座敢闯敢试的先锋城市，自觉置身于改革开放风口浪尖的前沿，以大气磅礴之势进入了全面改革和全方位开放的新阶段，一次次用生动的实践谱写光辉史册的新篇章；这座引领风气之先的国际城市，在波澜壮阔的全球一体化时代大潮中，风生水起乘势而为，以"先行先试"的锐气迎揽八面来风，一次次让世界听到响亮的中国声音。

在这本《印象厦门》中，您可以看见一座海岛嬗变成一座国际先锋城市的成长轨迹。这里坐拥广厦之门，方舆漫漫在时空中演绎无数次梦回与变迁；这里遇见碧山临海，叠翠碧波在亿万个晨曦与星光中盎然；这里镌满人文印记，人杰痕迹在讨海与信俗中世代巧琢；这里承载风物匠心，声影手作在味蕾中绽放传承不变初心；这里充盈创新活力，艺文纵横在包容并蓄与锐意开放中弄潮澎湃；这里安享诗意栖居，乐学宜居在博物开卷中生长闲趣与流韵。

厦门，在流金岁月和激情澎湃的打磨中，拥有了独特的城市节奏——既能飞快奔跑，又能自在娴静。

厦门，她聆听使命的召唤，她迎揽机缘的抉择，她无愧于历史的垂青。

厦门，她用一段段风云际会做青史告白。

Preface

Xiamen, the South Gate.

It is the gate for the reform and opening up of modern civilization of China to embrace the world and it is the gate for Chinese to explore the ocean by enduring great hardships with pioneering spirit and unremitting efforts.

When the clear and endless stream of Jiulong River flows down the Haimen Island, it turns around the Songyu Peninsula and winds its way to the vast ocean. Looking into the east, an array of islands like jade emerge at the other side of the vast expanse of water, which looks like a wave threshold separating the great river and giant ocean in the first rays of the morning sun.

"The South Gate! The South Gate!" The rosy dawn makes the blue water glittering. Estuary to the sea can be reached after going across the water area honored as "Jindaishui" of Gulangyu Island and stepping out the last "gate", which connects the Taiwan Strait and the Pacific Ocean...

Suddenly, it seems the space and time interweave. The meticulous and fantastic legends and realities fly past like rustling winds, which rouses the imagination about the exciting feelings for the ancestors who marched forward regardless of hardship to find this bay connecting the sea to the Southeast Asia. Perhaps, the flying gulls over the sea can still remember their expectations upon national rejuvenation with deep feelings.

The legend of Xiamen's name relies on the "men", which means "gate". From the external aspect, opening this gate can reach those minorities' places, bring in the trends and set up exchanges for the business ships, all of which has been acclaimed as the peak of perfection. From the internal aspect, it can connect Zhangzhou, Quanzhou and the vast inland, playing an important role as ferry and communication center for the sea, which shows its prominent geographic location.

This gate opens day and night. Xiamen locates at the key point by the sea, which stands as a gate between two sectors of inland and Southeast Asia. It is not only the source of the Central Plains' culture, but also the origin of South Fujian culture, which have accumulated the impact, collision and fusion of Chinese and Western culture, as well as engraved the inheritance, evolution and spread of the folk culture. The multi-source and composite humanistic society make Xiamen become the all-inclusive land, the cradle of new things, and eventually the great place with cultural diversity of South Fujian culture.

Xiamen, with the same character of the ocean, has always believed that every direction can be a road out of the inland. Endowed with broad momentum, endless energy and exploiting will by the ocean, this island city keeps opening the doors one by one by implementing the city's main function expansion across the island, across the surrounding cities and across the Taiwan Strait to go into the ocean, fly to the world and connect the globe.

This heroic city bearing a maritime dream has marked the glory again and again on this exuberant land with great momentum in the history of Chinese nation's great rejuvenation. This pioneering city takes the responsibility to stand at the frontier of the reform and opening up, enters the new stage of comprehensive reform and all-round opening up with great momentum, and writes a new chapter in the glorious history with vivid practice. This leading international city grasps the opportunity to develop as a pioneer in the magnificent era of global integration and takes the lead in embracing information, advice and other resources from outside to let the world hear the loud China's voice time after time.

Impression of Xiamen presents the growth story of an island evolving into an international pioneer city. As the gate of inland, Xiamen has gone through countless changes and transitions. Boasting green mountains and facing sea front, Xiamen always witnesses numerous emerald ripples twinkling in first rays of the morning sun as well as in starry nights. Abundant with human cultural relics, Xiamen has been enriched through fish trade and local customs generation after generation. Boasting incredible customs and ingenious craftsmanship, Xiamen has bloomed together with its unchanged traditions. A metropolis of creativity and vitality, Xiamen has become a leader in inclusivity, opening up for arts and literature. A place where poetic living is enjoyed, Xiamen is home for happy learning and leisurely living in abundant resources.

Xiamen, a city with unique rhythm polished by the golden years and great passions, can not only develop fast but also be carefree and tranquil.

Xiamen, a city follows the call of duty, embraces the choice of opportunity and lives up to the appreciation of history.

Xiamen, a city goes down in history through golden opportunities.

目录 CONTENTS

广厦之门 / 001
The Gate of Inland

碧山临海 / 017
Green Mountains and Blue Sea

人文印记 / 051
Cultural Impressions

风物匠心 / 087
Incredible Customs and Ingenious Craftsmanship

创新活力 / 113
Innovation and Vitality

诗意栖居 / 145
Poetic Living

ONE

广厦之门
THE GATE OF INLAND

厦门，这里坐拥**广厦之门**，方舆漫漫在时空中演绎无数次**梦回**与**变迁**。

As the gate of inland, Xiamen has gone through countless changes and transitions.

从地图上看，厦门岛安静地停泊在厦门湾中，三面是海岸，远离外海的厦门湾，微波荡漾，如同柔美似水的八幅裙裾。

厦门，并不是古都、古城，但其近代历史发轫甚早，早早就博得"闽海关第一口岸"的美誉，"五口通商"以后，这里更是"人民商贾，番船辏集"，"不减通都大邑之风"。

时空带着神秘而巨大的力量，推动着一切前行。作为近现代以来兴起的新型城市，厦门偏于东南一隅，面朝大海，被海风吹拂、被海浪冲击；她较早地接收西方文化，鹭江两岸奔流聚合，曲折挥洒，浪起云涌。

厦门人有岛民心态而无孤岛意识，开放包容而又斯文谦和。闽南文化与南洋文化碰撞兼容，开放意识标新融合，日积月累造就了厦门海洋文化的城市性格，她书写着与世界经济、贸易和文化密不可分的历史，呈现着共和国大厦之门改革开放的丰功伟绩。

日新月异的城市建设，让厦门这座城市充满盎然生机，她不只是本地人相濡以沫的鹭岛，更成为世界人心驰神往的海上花园。

Seen from the map, Xiamen Island berths in the Xiamen Bay quietly, which is surrounded by sea on three sides. Being far from the open seas, Xiamen Bay looks like the mellow petal dress with rippling waves.

Xiamen is not an ancient capital or ancient city, but its modern history sets afoot at a very early time. It has been honored as "the first port of Fujian customs" since a long time ago. After the "five-port trading treaty" was implemented, this place has been "crowded with businessmen and commercial ships", which demonstrates its "great charisma as a metropolis".

Time and space push all forward with a mysterious and great power. As a new city emerging from modern times, Xiamen is located in the southeast corner, facing the sea, blown by the sea breeze and beaten against by the sea waves. Hence, it can receive the Western culture earlier. Both sides of Lujiang (the Egret River) flow at a great speed and gather together with turning, unrestrained and rippling water.

Xiamen people have islander's mentality but no island consciousness, so they are open, tolerant, gentle and also modest and courteous. The culture of Fujian collides and merges with the culture of Southeast Asia, which is full of openness and innovation. As time passes by, Xiamen has cultivated its urban characteristic of maritime culture. It writes the history of the world economy, trade and culture, and presents the great achievements of reform and opening-up as the gate of the People's Republic of China.

The ever-changing city construction makes Xiamen full of vitality. It is not only the Egret Island for local people to rely on, but also a fascinating sea garden for people all around the world.

1 方舆 Geography

地理位置

厦门，犹如一颗明珠，镶嵌在中国的东南沿海。

厦门市位于福建省东端，是中国东南沿海重要的中心城市、国际性港口及风景旅游城市，素有"海上花园"的美誉；由本岛厦门岛、离岛鼓浪屿、西岸海沧半岛、北岸集美半岛、东岸翔安半岛、大小嶝岛、同安、九龙江等组成。

这里环境优美、气候宜人，是中国著名的风景旅游城市，以秀丽的山体为背景、开阔自由的海面为基底，"山、石、林、泉、湾、岛、岸"等丰富的自然资源为元素，形成张弛有致、极富韵律的"山海相融"景观特色，如诗如画。

Geographic Location

Xiamen inlays in the coastal area of the southeast China like a bright pearl.

Xiamen, a city in the southeast of Fujian Province, is an important center on the southeast coast of China, an international port and a popular tourist city. It is praised as a "garden on the sea". It consists of the main island Xiamen Island, offshore island Gulangyu Island, west coast Haicang Peninsula, north coast Jimei Peninsula, east coast Xiang'an Peninsula, Dadeng Island, Xiaodeng Island, Tong'an and Jiulong River and so on.

This city has a beautiful environment and a pleasant climate, which is China's famous tourist city with beautiful mountains as background and an open sea as the base. It has "mountains, stones, forests, springs, bays, islands and shores" and other rich natural resources elements, which forms an ordered and rhythmic landscape. The integration of the mountain and the sea makes the city poetic and picturesque.

地形地貌

厦门市的地形由西北向东南倾斜。西北部多中低山，位于同安与安溪交界处的云顶山海拔1175.2米，为全市最高峰。从西北往东南，依次分布高丘、低丘、阶地、海积平原和滩涂，南面是厦门岛和鼓浪屿。

厦门岛是福建省的第四大岛，1955年建成海堤后成为半岛。厦门岛的地形南高北低，南部多丘陵，最高峰云顶岩海拔339.6米，北部为海拔200米以下的低丘和阶地。

厦门海域包括厦门港、外港区、马銮湾、同安湾、九龙江河口区和东侧水道。厦门港外有大金门、小金门、大担、二担等岛屿横列，内有厦门岛、鼓浪屿等岛屿屏障，是天然的避风良港。

Topographic Features

The terrain of Xiamen tilts from northwest to southeast. There are many middle and low mountains in the northwest. Yunding Mountain, the highest peak in the city, located at the junction of Tong'an and Anxi, is 1175.2 meters above sea level. From northwest to southeast, it follows the distribution of high hills, low hills, terraces, sea plains and tidal flats. Xiamen Island and Gulangyu Island are in the south.

Xiamen Island is the fourth largest island in Fujian Province. It became a peninsula after the completion of the seawall in 1955. The topography of the Xiamen Island is high in the south and low in the north. More hills are in the south. The highest peak Yundingyan is 339.6 meters above the sea level. In the north, there are low hills and terraces below 200 meters.

Xiamen waters include Xiamen Port, Outer Harbor Area, Maluan Bay, Tong'an Bay, Jiulong River's estuary area and the waterway on the east side. Outside the Xiamen Port, Big Kinmen, Little Kinmen, Dadan, Erdan and other islands are arranged in a horizontal line. Inside, it has Xiamen Island, Gulangyu Island and other island barriers, making it a good natural port protected from storms.

行政区划

厦门市辖思明、湖里、集美、海沧、同安和翔安 6 个行政区；2019 年年末，厦门市常住人口达 429 万人，以汉族为主，还有畲族、回族等部分少数民族；厦门还是著名的侨乡，拥有众多的侨胞、归侨及侨眷。

Administrative Division

Xiamen City has six administrative districts including Siming, Huli, Jimei, Haicang, Tong'an and Xiang'an. By the end of 2019, the resident population of Xiamen has reached 4.29 million, the majority being is Han people. There are also some minorities such as She and Hui. Xiamen is also the famous hometown of overseas Chinese with a sizeable proportion of overseas Chinese, returned overseas Chinese and relatives of overseas Chinese.

广厦之门
THE GATE OF INLAND

	1	
2	3	4
	5	6

1. 思明区　Siming District
2. 湖里区　Huli District
3. 集美区　Jimei District
4. 海沧区　Haicang District
5. 同安区　Tong'an District
6. 翔安区　Xiang'an District

城市元素
City Element

● 市花

"不拘墙头、路旁，无论草坡、石隙，只要阳光常年有，春夏秋冬，都是你的花期，呵，抬头是你，低头是你，闭上眼睛还是你……"这是厦门著名女诗人舒婷的名篇《日光岩下的三角梅》。

三角梅是厦门的市花，古时称"九重葛"，北方多叫"叶小花""三角花"，香港则用译音"宝巾"称之。

三角梅四季常开，刚柔并济，朴实无华；它既可盆栽也可地植，生机蓬勃，象征着厦门人"爱拼才会赢"的奋斗精神。

City Flower

"No matter where you are, on the top of wall, by the roadside, on a grass slope or in the crack of a stone, you can always blossom in the four seasons as long as there is sunshine. Ah, I can see you when I look up, I can feel you when I lower my head and I can dream of you when I close my eyes..." This is selected from the famous work *Bougainvillea under Sunlight Rock* from the famous female poet Shu Ting in Xiamen.

Bougainvillea is the city flower of Xiamen, which was called "Bougainvillea spectabilis Willd" in ancient times. In the north, it is often called "Yexiaohua" or "Triangle Flower". In Hong Kong it is called "Bougan" in transliteration.

Bougainvillea can blossom in four seasons. It couples hardness with softness and shows simple and unadorned features. It can be planted in the pot or in the field. It is very vibrant, which symbolizes the struggling spirit of "no pain no gain" of Xiamen people.

● 市树

凤凰木亦称"红楹""火树"，原产于非洲，属豆科落叶乔木，长成后可高达20米。由于"叶如飞凰之羽，花若丹凤之冠"，故取名凤凰。凤凰木花开之时，花瓣或鲜红或明橙，映衬着鲜绿色的羽状复叶，更显富丽堂皇，被誉为世界上色彩最鲜艳的树木。热情、浪漫的凤凰木最能勾起人们的火样情怀，象征厦门的风貌、厦门人民的性格和厦门经济特区的腾飞景象。

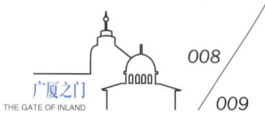

● 市鸟

　　厦门古名"鹭岛"，白鹭是厦门的象征。

　　白鹭属鸟纲鹭科，为世界珍稀鸟类。厦门分布有小白鹭、中白鹭、大白鹭、中国鹭和岩鹭，这也是至今我国记录的仅有的五种。由于它们体羽除岩鹭为暗灰色外，均为雪白色，因此，人们通常统称这五种鹭为白鹭。

　　白鹭翱翔蓝天，成为厦门一道动感的风景线。

City Bird

　　Xiamen's ancient name is "Egret Island". Egret is the symbol of Xiamen.

　　Egret belongs to the Ardeidae family, and it is the world's rare bird. In Xiamen, Egretta garzetta, Egretta intermedia, Ardea alba, Chinese egret and Egretta sacra distribute here, which are the only five species documented in China at present. Besides Egretta sacra with grey feather, others are all white. Thus, people usually refer to these five species all as egrets.

　　Egrets soar in the blue sky and become a dynamic tourist attraction in Xiamen.

City Tree

　　Delonix Regia, also called "Red Jacaranda" or "Flame Tree". It originates in Africa, which belongs to leguminous deciduous trees. It can grow up to 20 meters. As the "leaves like flying phoenix feathers and flowers like the crown of the red phoenix", it is named after phoenix. When Delonix Regia blossoms, its petals are bright red or bright orange, which seems to be more gorgeous against the green feather-shaped compound leaves. Passionate and romantic Delonix Regia can evoke people's torrid feelings. It symbolizes the style and feature of Xiamen, Xiamen people's character and the prosperous scene of Xiamen Special Economic Zone.

2 梦回 Change

两三千年前，厦门岛及其周围生活着闽越族人。

晋朝太康三年（282年）于此置同安县，这也是厦门历史上第一次由中央政府设立行政机构。此后经唐、五代、宋、元的建设与治理，到明洪武二十年（1387年）始筑"厦门城"——意寓国家大厦之门，"厦门"之名自此列入史册。

明中叶以后东南地区私人海上贸易勃兴，厦门开始从军事据点演化成贸易重镇。明末郑成功占据厦门作为抗清基地，其后清廷平定台湾，划定厦门为闽台贸易的重要枢纽，奠定了厦门与台湾之特殊关系。

清代《厦门志》序文里写道："厦门处泉、漳之交，扼台湾之要，为东南门户。"从历史看，厦门自筑城起即为海防御敌之门，后又成为郑成功"通洋裕国"之门，再后来又成为商品进出口和华侨进出之门，所谓"国家大厦之门"，名副其实。

早在康熙年间，清政府就在厦门设立海关。此后的几百年里，厦门逐渐成为我国对外交通贸易的四大港口之一。至19世纪中叶，厦门被划为通商口岸，容许外国人在厦门进行通商及传教活动。

1895年日本割占台湾岛，从此厦门失去台湾对外贸易转口港地位。但由于东南亚殖民经济发展，对劳动力需求方殷，厦门因此成为人力输出港，变为闽省华侨集散地，这刺激了厦门的城市发展，厦门也因此成为"海洋中国"的典型城市。

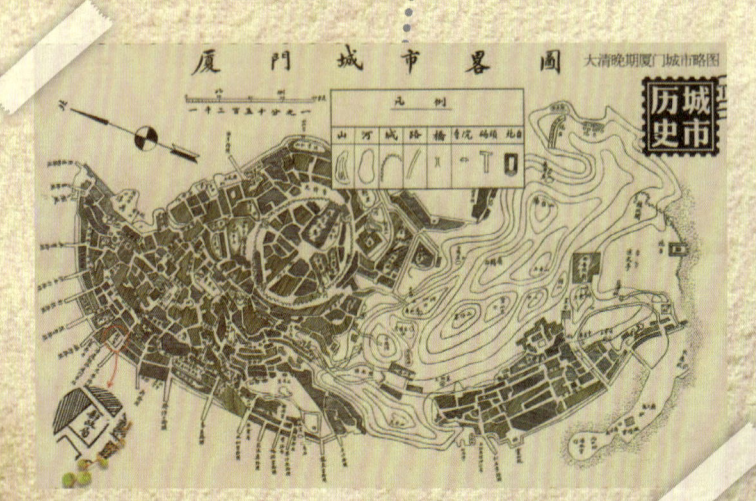

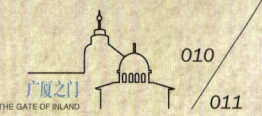

据统计，1949 年，厦鼓二岛人口 20 万；1980 年为 49 万；2019 年年底常住人口达到 429 万。短短一甲子的时间，人口净增三百余万。一座小城市迅速成长为大城市。

About two or three thousand years ago, Fujian people lived in Xiamen Island and its surrounding area.

Tong'an County was set up in the 3rd year of Taikang of the Jin Dynasty (282), which was the first administrative agency in history set up in Xiamen by the central government. After the governance of the Tang Dynasty, Five Dynasties, the Song Dynasty and the Yuan Dynasty, "Xiamen City" was firstly built in the 20th year of Hongwu of the Ming Dynasty (1387), meaning the gate of the nation. The name of "Xiamen" has been remembered in history since then.

After the middle of the Ming Dynasty, private maritime trade developed vigorously in Southeast China, and Xiamen evolved into a trade center from a military base. By the end of the Ming Dynasty, Zheng Chenggong occupied Xiamen as an anti-Qing base, and then the Qing court put down Taiwan and designated Xiamen as an important hub for trade between Fujian and Taiwan, laying a special relationship between Xiamen and Taiwan.

It is said in the preface of *The Annals of Xiamen* that "Xiamen is located at the intersection of Quanzhou and Zhangzhou, occupying an important military position against Taiwan and being the gate of Southeast China". From the historical perspective, Xiamen was the gate for coastal defense and resisting enemy ever since its establishment, and later became the gate for "connecting with foreign countries and enriching China" promoted by Zheng Chenggong. Then it became the gate for import and export and for overseas Chinese to get into and out of China. It is worthy of the name "Gate of China".

As early as in the Kangxi Era, the Qing government had set up customs in Xiamen. In the past several hundreds of years, Xiamen has gradually become one of the four main ports of China's foreign communication and trade. Till the middle of the 19th century, Xiamen was listed as a trading port to allow foreigners to conduct business and missionary activities in this city.

In 1895 when Japan occupied Taiwan, Xiamen did not serve as the entrepot of Taiwan's foreign trade any longer. However, due to the development of colonial economy in Southeast Asia, the demand for labor increased substantially. Then Xiamen became a labor output port and changed into the gathering place of Fujian overseas Chinese, thus stimulating the urban development of Xiamen, and making Xiamen become a typical city of "Ocean China".

According to statistics, the population of Xiamen Island and Gulangyu Island reached 200,000 in 1949; it reached 490,000 in 1980; the resident population reached 4.29 million at the end of 2019. The population increased by more than 3 million in sixty years. A small city has developed rapidly into a big city.

3 变迁 / Transition

茶马古道

　　山间铃响马帮来，古道密林幽深。

　　厦门同安区、泉州安溪县龙门镇与南安市翔云镇一带，有一条"茶马古道"，从宋元直至民国时期，年复一年地在三地之间的茂林深山里来回运送山货海产。

　　这条古道，《厦门市志》《同安县志》中均有记载："自同安城关经上埔，曲折往西北，经西源、半岭、过县境内海拔900米的东岭至安溪县的龙门，全长20里，宽4尺，鹅卵石路面，多坡。"

　　山区生产的山货经茶马古道运到位于同安西溪上游的草仔市码头装船，通过"海上丝绸之路"销往各地；从"海丝"运来的火柴等洋货，经草仔市码头，肩挑马驮运往山区。

Ancient Tea-Horse Road

　　Caravans come as bell rings in mountain, and ancient road stretches to the depth of dense forest.

　　There is an "ancient tea-horse road" in Tong'an District of Xiamen, Longmen Town in Anxi County of Quanzhou and Xiangyun Town of Nan'an City, transporting mountain products and seafood between the forests and mountains of the three places year after year from the Song and Yuan Dynasties to the period of the Republic of China.

　　This ancient road is recorded in both *Xiamen Shi Zhi* and *Tong'an Xian Zhi*: "The road starts from Tong'an City, turns to the northwest via Shangpu, and reached Longmen Town of Anxi County through Xiyuan, Banling and Dongling at an elevation of 900 meters. The 4-chi-wide (about 1.33 meters) pebble road is full of slopes and covers a complete length of 20 li (about 6.21 miles)."

　　Mountain products are transported to the Caozai Port, which is located in the upstream of Xixi River in Tong'an via the ancient tea-horse road, shipped at the port and then sold to other places through "Maritime Silk Road". The foreign goods such as matches which are shipped from "Maritime Silk Road" are transported to the mountains by means of labor and horses via the Caozai Port.

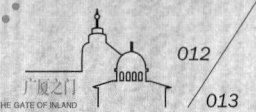

五口通商

1842年，中国的五个沿海城市——广州、厦门、福州、宁波和上海被辟为通商口岸，史称五口通商。厦门于清道光二十三年九月十一日（1843年11月2日）正式开埠。

清道光二十五年（1845年），时任福州将军兼闽海关的敬穆向道光皇帝所上奏折中这样诉说厦门开埠后的情形："该夷除贩运洋货外，兼运洋布洋棉，其物冲积于厦口。内地之商贩，皆在厦门运入各府，其质既美，其价复廉，民间之买洋布洋棉者，十室而九空。"

开埠以后，厦门的贸易对象从东亚、东南亚扩大到了西方。

Five Trading Ports

In 1842, five of China's coastal cities opened as trading ports, namely Guangzhou, Xiamen, Fuzhou, Ningbo and Shanghai, and became known as the "five trading ports". On September 11 of the 23rd year of Daoguang of the Qing Dynasty (November 2, 1843), Xiamen was officially opened.

In the 25th year of Daoguang of the Qing Dynasty (1845), Jing Mu, then general of Fuzhou and Director of Fujian Customs, presented a memorial to the emperor, which stated the case of Xiamen after the commercial port opening: "People transport not only foreign goods, but also foreign cloth and cotton, which will all piled up in Xiamen Port. Inland businessmen transport goods from Xiamen Port to various regions through the country. The goods in trade are of good quality and sold at a cheap price. Most stores that sell foreign cloth and foreign cotton are emptied by eager buyers."

After being opened as a trading port, Xiamen started to have trade exchanges with Western countries besides East Asian and Southeast Asian countries.

经济特区

　　1980年，国务院正式批复设立厦门经济特区，1981年10月15日，厦门经济特区湖里出口加工区正式破土建设。1984年2月，厦门经济特区从湖里2.5平方公里扩大至全岛131平方公里。2010年6月，厦门经济特区范围扩大到厦门全市，将岛外的集美、海沧、同安、翔

安4区纳入经济特区范围。此次扩区，厦门经济特区的面积扩大到1573平方公里，"长大"11倍。

"厦迎五洲客，门泊万里船"，经济特区的设立赋予厦门改革开放"试验田"和"排头兵"的重大使命。厦门三十多年的历史进程始终脱离不开"以开放促改革、以开放促发展"这一主线。今天，厦门已经成为"一带一路"重要支点城市，成为两岸交流合作的前沿平台，成为文明和谐的幸福家园。

Special Economic Zone

In 1980, the establishment of Xiamen Special Economic Zone was officially approved by the State Council, and the construction of Huli Export Processing Zone in Xiamen Special Economic Zone was officially started on October 15, 1981. In February 1984, Xiamen Special Economic Zone was expanded from an area of 2.5 square kilometers of Huli to 131 square kilometers of the whole island. In June 2010, Xiamen Special Economic Zone was expanded to the whole Xiamen City, and four districts outside Xiamen Island including Jimei, Haicang, Tong'an and Xiang'an were included into the zone. After this expansion, the area of Xiamen Special Economic Zone reached 1,573 square kilometers, 11 times larger than before.

"Xiamen welcomes people from all over the world and ships across thousands of miles." The establishment of Special Economic Zone granted Xiamen major missions of reform and opening up, namely, to be the "experimental field" and the "vanguard". Xiamen's historical process of thirty years has closely connected with the direction of "promoting reform and development through opening up". Today, Xiamen has developed into an important supporting city of the Belt and Road Initiative, an advanced platform for cross-strait exchanges and cooperation, and a civilized and harmonious home.

"一带一路"

中国提出共建"丝绸之路经济带"和"21世纪海上丝绸之路"的倡议，肩负时代使命的厦门经济特区锁定"一带一路"新目标，以更加从容自信的态度积极应对国际竞争，加快构建21世纪海上丝绸之路上重要的枢纽城市。

"一带一路"拉开中国经济建设发展新常态下转型升级的大幕，围绕这一目标，厦门在口岸、贸易、投资和华侨华人、人文历史、民间交流上运用独特的优势，创新合作机制，拓宽合作领域，叠加自贸试验区效应，高位对接全球高新科技的风潮和产业转移的浪潮；打造国际化营商环境，有效探索合乎全球经济一体化的"仿真国际投资环境"；主动走出国门招商引资，进一步开放基础设施建设、临港产业发展的合作领域，誓将这座海上城市打造成"新海丝"的支点城市。

The Belt and Road Initiative

China has proposed the initiative of co-building "Silk Road Economic Belt" and "the 21st Century Maritime Silk Road". Xiamen Special Economic Zone, bearing the mission of the era, has focused on the new goals of "Belt and Road" to deal with international competition with a more confident attitude and to facilitate the construction of the important hub city of the 21st Century Maritime Silk Road.

The "Belt and Road" has started the transformation and upgrading of China's economic construction and development under the new normal. Focusing on this target and taking its unique advantages in port, trade, investment and overseas Chinese, humanistic history and people-to-people exchanges, Xiamen has innovated cooperation mechanism, expanded cooperation fields, and multiplied the effects of the FTZ (Free Trade Zone) pilot area to match the global high-tech wave and industrial transfer wave. Xiamen has also built an international business environment to effectively explore the "simulation of an international investment environment" in line with global economic integration, and has taken the initiative to attract foreign investment and further open the cooperation areas in infrastructure construction and port-centric industrial development so as to build this city on the sea into a supporting city of the "New Maritime Silk Road".

2

Boasting green mountains and facing sea front, Xiamen always witnesses numerous emerald ripples twinkling in first rays of the morning sun as well as in starry nights.

TWO
碧山临海
GREEN MOUNTAINS AND BLUE SEA

厦门,这里遇见**碧山临海**,叠翠碧波在亿万个晨曦与星光中盎然。

西方著名哲学家亚里士多德曾说过:"大自然的每一个领域都是美妙绝伦的。"

一抹汪洋,一座岛屿,一片青山,一池碧潭,一缕馥郁,一树嫣红……厦门,这颗镶嵌在中国东南沿海的璀璨明珠,恰是大自然的绝美馈赠。

这里环境优美,气候宜人,大海是她的主旋律,潮卷浪涌之间勾勒出岛城的无限风情;这里空气清新,草木葳蕤,苍翠是她的主色调,青山碧海之中藏匿着"海上花园"的独特气质;这里燕语莺啼,诗意盎然,旖旎的自然风光与亭台楼阁的园林之美交相辉映,一步一移皆是胜景。

这是一个经得起时间沉淀的城市。"城在海上、海在城中",青山、碧海、蓝天、红花、白鹭,这些千百年的景象始终未变。恰如生长在鼓浪屿的著名诗人舒婷所描述:"我很幸运,生长在这样一个南方岛屿,春夏秋冬,日日夜夜,与绿树鲜花呼吸与共。"

Aristotle, a famous Western philosopher, once said: "Every realm of nature is marvelous."

Enjoying the sea, island, green mountain, blue lake, strong fragrance and flowers, and so on, Xiamen is a beautiful gift of nature, a shining pearl on the southeast coast of China.

Xiamen possesses a beautiful environment and a pleasant climate, in which everything is around the sea, showing its infinite style by the waves, ebb and flow. Here the air is fresh with luxuriant vegetation, accompanied by its green main hue and unique temperament of "garden on the sea" surrounded by green mountains and blue sea. Swallows and nightingales are everywhere in the poetic environment. The beautiful natural scenery and beauty of gardens represented by pavilions, add radiance and charm to each other, so every piece of this land is a wonderful scenery.

This is a city that can withstand the test of time. "The city above the sea and the sea embraces the city", the beauties including green mountain, blue sea, blue sky, red flowers and egrets are still charming after thousands of years. Just as Shu Ting, who grew up in Gulangyu Island, described, "I am very fortunate to have grown up on such a beautiful southern island, so I can breathe with the green trees and flowers every day and night through the four seasons of each year."

1 碧波
Emerald Ripples

鹭江

　　鼓浪屿和厦门岛之间的海域,宽600米,因海面上常有许多美丽优雅的白鹭盘旋飞翔,故称为鹭江。

　　被誉为"厦门外滩"的鹭江道,沿线的骑楼老建筑和古典建筑镌刻着百年历史,舒展着洁白身躯与鹭江碧波交相辉映的演武大桥日夜枕海听涛,对岸还有琴声悠扬的鼓浪小岛,形成鹭江两岸一道独特的风景线。在此岸,看见云雾里的小岛轮廓如同诗画般浪漫;于彼岸,望得见人潮涌动的步行街点缀在霓虹闪烁的高屋楼宇间那股新旧交织的繁华景象。恰是这道鹭江,为对岸好似"不食人间烟火"的鼓浪屿笼上一层朦胧的面纱,非得跨过这不近不远的数百米才可一睹风采。

　　连缀演武大桥、海沧大桥、杏林大桥三点的鹭江夜游,为游人海上欣赏绚丽夜景提供了全新的视角,鹭江两岸的一灯一火,都在那摇晃着的波涛中沉醉心底。

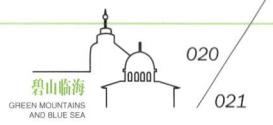

Lujiang

The sea between Gulangyu Island and Xiamen Island is 600 meters wide, and called Lujiang (the Egret River) for the fact that many beautiful and elegant egrets fly around.

Lujiang Ave is known as the "Xiamen Bund". The arcade old buildings and classical buildings along the road are engraved with a hundred years of history. Yanwu Bridge and Lujiang add charms to each other, and the other side of the river is Gulangyu Island where the beautiful piano sounds flow around. All these sceneries form a unique landscape of the two sides of Lujiang. On one side, the outline of the island is romantic and poetic. On the other side, the bustling scene is formed by a Pedestrian Street and neon-flashing high buildings. It is exactly this Lujiang that covers a hazy veil on the "other-worldly" Gulangyu Island, so people have to cross over about hundreds of meters to enjoy its beauty.

Lujiang night tour including Yanwu Bridge, Haicang Bridge and Xinglin Bridge provides visitors a new perspective to enjoy the magnificent night view by the sea. The lights on both sides of this river intoxicate visitors' heart along with the great waves.

筼筜湖

筼筜湖，旧称筼筜港，相传古时候筼筜港北岸种满了名为"筼筜"的巨竹林，绵延数里，故港以竹名；筼筜港原与大海相通，20世纪70年代围海造田，筑起了从浮屿到东渡的西堤，从此，筼筜港成为内湖，湖内水域面积约1.7平方公里。

"筼筜夜色"便是从古景"筼筜渔火"演变而来。过去，每当夜幕降临之时，筼筜港里的渔船回港休憩，水面掀起阵阵涟漪，一船一灯便随波摇曳，水中的倒影亦一明一灭随之闪烁，景致奇特，故名"筼筜渔火"。如今，夜晚的筼筜湖虽已无渔火，"筼筜夜色"却毫不逊色——衬着湖中台地白鹭洲，筼筜湖背靠人民会堂，坐拥湖堤沿岸成群楼宇，堤岸边的步行道与一座座小桥投射下的星星点点如同往日的渔火般，于水面摇曳飘忽，风情未减。这里，是厦门新旧城区的中心带，见证着厦门发生着的巨变。

Yundang Lake

Yundang Lake is originally called Yundang Harbor which is named after a bamboo's name, because it's said that in ancient times a large bamboo forest which was called "Yundang" at the length of several li (1 li = 0.31 mile) was planted on the northern bank of Yundang harbor. The harbor was connected to the sea before, but due to reclaiming land from the sea in the 1970s, the west embankment was built from Fuyu to Dongdu. Since then, Yundang Harbor became an endorheic lake with a water area of 1.7 square kilometers.

"Yundang Night View" evolves from the ancient scene "Yundang lights on fishing boats". In the past, whenever the night fell, the fishing boats of Yundang Harbor returned to the harbor to rest. Bursts of ripples are set off on the surface of water, boats and lights swaying with waves. The reflection on the water also flickers with the boats and lights. This fantastic scenery is called "Yundang lights on fishing boats". Nowadays, although there is no light on fishing boats on Yundang Lake at night, the "Yundang Night View" is still wonderful. At night, Bailuzhou in the center of the lake, the People's Hall at the back of the lake, a large number of high buildings and footpaths along the lake banks, and the bridges all flicker on the water just like the lights in the past, wonderful as before. Here is the center of the new and old city districts of Xiamen, witnessing the great changes in Xiamen.

白城沙滩

如果说每片沙滩都有独特的旋律，环岛南路的白城沙滩应该是首优雅的蓝调小曲。

从厦门大学东部的白城校门出来，走过一座弧形虹桥似的人行天桥，便来到这片蜿蜒数百米的弧形海湾。凭借优越独特的地理位置和便捷的交通，白城海水浴场一直是老厦门人游泳、戏水的好去处，这片沙滩也颇受厦大学子及游人的青睐。许多明信片上都能见到的那两块大礁石，恰在白城沙滩岸边，巨大的礁盘，低潮时露出，高潮时淹没，潮起潮落间竟不知不觉成了一处小景致。

Baicheng Beach

If every beach is said to embody a unique melody, Baicheng Beach in Island Ring Blvd (S) should be an elegant Blues song.

Walking out of the Baicheng Gate in the eastern Xiamen University and passing through the footbridge resembling a curved rainbow, you will see the curved bay meandering for hundreds of meters. Owing to the excellent and unique geographical location and convenient transportation, Baicheng bathing beach is always a preferred place for the indigenous Xiamen people to swim and play. This beach is also a favourite place of students in Xiamen University as well as other tourists. Two big reefs you may find on many postcards are also located beside the bank of Baicheng Beach. The huge reef is exposed when tide is low and immersed when the tide is high, which has unconsciously become a small scenic spot with the ebb and flow.

观音山沙滩

　　观音山沙滩位于厦门岛东部，背靠环岛路，面朝厦门东海域。天高云阔，是观音山的背景色，金沙与碧海相接，总能拍出许多绝美的相片。在这片广阔的沙滩上，与三五好友一同放飞风筝，听海鸥声声、浪花阵阵，享受这无与伦比的海天美景；或干脆解放天性，提着鞋子一脚踏入温热柔软的沙滩，感受这片沙滩释放的激情与活力。

　　同许多温婉的沙滩不同，观音山沙滩以热烈和奔放为主旋律，著名的沙雕文化公园、厦门观音山梦幻水陆世界度假区均坐落于此。每年，观音山沙滩还会举办国际排联世界沙滩排球巡回赛、沙滩音乐节，将放飞心情、纵情狂欢的主题升华到极致。

Guanyinshan Beach

　　Guanyinshan Beach is located in the eastern Xiamen Island against Island Ring Blvd, facing the eastern stretch of Xiamen sea area. The high sky forms the background of Guanyinshan and the integration of the golden sand and green sea is perfect for taking photos. On this wide beach, you can enjoy the unparalleled beauty of the sky and sea, either by flying kites with several friends or listening to the sound of sea gull and waves. Alternatively, you can fully relax yourself through walking on the soft beach with shoes in hand to fully experience the enthusiasm and energy the beach releases.

　　Guanyinshan Beach, different from many gentle beaches, is mainly well-known for its enthusiasm and exuberance, where the famous Sand Sculpture Cultural Park and Guanyinshan Fantasy Beach Resort Area are also located. Moreover, Guanyinshan Beach holds the International Beach Volleyball Competition and Beach Music Festival every year, which fully expresses the theme of relaxing your mind and living it up.

五缘湾

　　五缘湾位于厦门岛东北部，厦门机场和翔安隧道之间，横卧于湾内的五座圆拱大桥是其醒目标志——象征着天缘、地缘、日缘、月缘、人缘的五座拱桥与其倒影构成"五圆"，谐音"五缘"，寓意人与天地、日月和谐共存。这里是厦门岛内唯一集水景、温泉、植被、湿地、海湾等多种自然资源于一体的风水宝地。

　　"启航"是屹立在五缘湾内湾的标志性雕塑，这座全国极为少见的大型海上铜雕展现渔民坚韧不拔、斩风劈浪的力量之美。雕塑身后，是中国东南地区最大最成熟的五缘湾游艇港，拥有351个水上泊位。因水质良好，空气清新，景观开阔，常年有风，这里被航海界人士称赞为"全球少见的帆船运动基地"，更有"最美帆船港"的美誉。中国（厦门）国际游艇展览会、中国俱乐部杯帆船赛、海峡杯帆船赛等知名会展赛事均在此举办。

Wuyuan Bay

Wuyuan Bay is located in the northeast of the Xiamen Island between the Xiamen Airport and Xiang'an Tunnel. The five arched bridges lying in the bay are the clear symbols of Wuyuan Bay, which represent the Yuan (relationships) with the heaven, land, sun, moon and human beings respectively. Together with their shadows in the water, they form "Wuyuan" (five circles), a homonym of Wuyuan (five relationships), which implies that human beings co-exist with the heaven, land, sun and moon. This is also the only treasured place in the Xiamen Island integrating water scenes, hot springs, vegetation, wetlands and bay.

"Qihang (Setting Sail)", the large maritime copper statue rarely seen in the country, is the landmark sculpture standing in the inner Wuyuan Bay, representing the beauty of fishermen's power with perseverance and courage. Behind the sculpture lies the Wuyuan Bay yacht harbor, the largest and the most mature one in the southeast China, which has 351 water berths. Owing to the good-quality water, fresh air, wide landscape and year-long wind, this harbor is praised as "the worldwide rare sailing base" and even gains the reputation of "the most beautiful sailing harbor". China (Xiamen) International Boat Show, China Club Challenge Match and Strait Cup Yacht Competition and other famous exhibitions and competitions are held here.

杏林湾

　　杏林湾，被称作"厦门西湖"，水域面积6.9平方公里，由上游的后溪流域汇聚而成，拥有天然海湾、温泉和湿地资源。它坐落在集美半岛的西边，与集美新城依傍而生，北经孙厝、兑山，西经西亭、董任直至杏林湾，形成一个小小的内海海湾。据闻，集美孙厝的人们都亲切地称它为"西海"或"西港"。

　　在环杏林湾绿道上，石板小路与木栈道散发着古朴清幽的气息。湾畔风景旖旎，绿荫环抱，午后时分或是骑自行车，或是漫步其间，花红柳绿，流水潺潺，自然风光尽收眼底，两侧高楼与自然美景的完美融合更给杏林湾畔带来颇有城市现代感的别致之美。

Xinglin Bay

　　Xinglin Bay, regarded as the "West Lake in Xiamen", covers a water area of 6.9 square kilometers and is formed by the confluence of Houxi river basin in the upstream, which owns the natural resources of bay, hot springs and wet lands. Located in the west of Jimei Peninsular and adjacent to the Jimei Xincheng, it is a small gulf in the inland sea bay caused by its location for passing through Suncuo, Duishan in the north and Xiting, Dongren and Xinglin Bay in the west. It is said that people in Jimei Suncuo all lovingly call it as "West Sea" or "West Harbor".

　　On the green road surrounding Xinglin Bay, both the stone path and plank road create an ancient and quiet atmosphere. The scenery of the bay is extremely beautiful and surrounded by green trees. In the afternoon, either by riding a bike or strolling, you can enjoy the extraordinary natural scenes of the red flowers, green trees and gurgling water. The perfect combination of the high buildings and natural scenes brings unique beauty for Xinglin Bay featuring urban modernization.

2 叠翠
Emerald Mountains

日光岩

　　日光岩，又名晃岩，位于鼓浪屿中部偏南的龙头山顶端，两块巨石一竖一横相倚而立，海拔92.7米，为鼓浪屿最高峰。"日""光"二字合为"晃"，相传1647年郑成功到此，觉得它的景色胜于日本的日光山，改其名为"日光岩"。

　　俗话说"不登日光岩不算到厦门"。日光岩顶峰上有一直径40多米的巨石，凌空耸立，成为厦门的象征。民族英雄郑成功收复台湾前，曾屯兵于此，留下许多动人的传说。山上巨石嵯峨，草木葱郁，拥有"一片瓦""鹭江龙窟""古避暑洞""龙头山寨""水操台""百米高台"等胜景。历代文人石刻题咏甚多，为名岩增添古风异彩。

Sunlight Rock

　　Sunlight Rock, nicknamed as Huang Rock, lies on the top of Longtou Mountain in south-central Gulangyu Island. Two rocks lean against each other. It is 92.7 meters above sea level, which is the highest of Gulangyu Island. In Chinese, the combination of sun and light means "Huang (dazzling)". It is said that when Zheng Chenggong arrived here in 1647, he thought it was much more beautiful than Nikko (sunlight) Mountain in Japan and renamed it "Sunlight Rock".

　　There is a saying that "if you haven't ascended Sunlight Rock, you haven't really been to Xiamen". Perched atop Sunlight Rock is a gigantic stone with a diameter of over 40 meters, and the towering creation of nature becomes the symbol of Xiamen. Moreover, it was where Zheng Chenggong (often known abroad as Koxinga) stationed his troops before he recovered Taiwan from Dutch occupation. Many impressive legends about him were left here. The mountain has numerous gigantic stones, green grass, trees, and many famous scenes such as "Yipian Wa", "Lujiang Longku", "Ancient Summer Cave", "Longtou Fortress", "Water Control Platform", and "Platform over One Hundred Meters". Many stone inscriptions and poems from ancient scholars add ancient splendor to this famous rock.

五老峰

五老峰是位于南普陀寺后面的五座山峰，依次为一峰（钟峰）、二峰、三峰（中峰）、四峰、五峰（鼓峰），峥嵘凌空，时有白云缭绕，云下丛林葱郁，宛如五位须发皆白、历尽人间沧桑的老人面天盘坐，丛树若须，云雾似袖，翘首遥望茫茫大海，故名"五老凌霄"。

五老凌霄以其挺拔秀奇著称。山上林木葱郁，奇石嶙峋，洞壑幽深，岩泉清洌。若从藏经阁后面登阶，可见山坡上镌刻着"五老峰"三字，迎面巨石上刻着特大的"佛"字，高4米多，宽3米多，笔画丰满有力，粗犷豪放，似乎大笔一挥而就。这是清光绪三十一年（1905年）振慧和尚所书，吸引了许多善男信女来此烧香磕头。

Wulao Peaks

Wulao Peaks are five peaks behind the Nanputuo Temple, which are the first peak (Bell Peak), second peak, third peak (Middle Peak), fourth peak and fifth peak (Drum Peak) in order. The five peaks stand high into the sky, which appear to be verdant against the surrounded clouds sometimes. They resemble the elder people with white beards and hair who have already experienced the vicissitudes of life and are sitting cross-legged facing the sky and looking at the boundless sea, with the trees as their beard and the clouds and fog as their sleeves. Therefore, the five peaks get the name of "Wulao Lingxiao (five elder people soaring into the sky)".

Wulao Lingxiao is famous for its straight and unique scenery. On the mountain can lush forests, rugged stones, deep caves and clean spring water be found. If stepping up from the back of the Zangjing Ge (Cabinet of Buddhist Scriptures), you can see the hill engraved with "Wulao peaks". Opposite to it, a big "Fo (Buddha)" character is engraved on the stone with a height of 4 meters and a width of 3 meters, whose strokes seem to be powerful and smoothly finished by a single brushstroke. It is written by Zhenhui Monk in the 31st year of Guangxu of the Qing Dynasty (1905), attracting many men and women to come and pray.

东坪山

　　东坪山位于厦门岛南部，是国内难得一见的城市中央山地公园。从厦大公寓附近的书法广场穿越东坪山到东芳山庄，全程约11公里，一路绿树成荫，沿着蜿蜒曲折的林道抵达山顶后，便能远眺大海，沿途还可在"怪坡"体验"汽车熄火自动上坡"的奇妙现象。

　　"含蕊红三叶，临风艳一城"，四季都不忘盛放的三角梅在这座山的怀抱中甚是夺目，漫山遍野，绚烂如霞。这便是东坪山上的厦门市花园"梅海岭"，园内共栽种三角梅1万多株，共有50多个品种。

　　穿过梅海岭，便可到达东坪山水库，波光粼粼中，可以望见岸边垂钓的人们，周边的农家乐、山间的小资民宿更是吸引众多游人来访。这似乎闻得到淡淡海风的斑驳绿荫，正成为人们放松身心、返璞归真的不二之选。

Dongping Mountain

　　Dongping Mountain, lying in the southern Xiamen Island, is the mountain park in the city center, which is rarely seen in China. Along the 11 kilometers from the Calligraphy Square near Xiamen University Student Dormitory to Dongfang Mountain Villa through Dongping Mountain, trees stand in lines. On reaching the peak by walking from the twisted passages in the trees, you can enjoy the splendid sea. Moreover, you can also experience the incredible phenomenon along the way—"going up automatically without the engine powering on" in the "Mysterious Slope".

　　"The numerous flowers impress all the citizens when wind sends them in all directions." Bougainvillea, blooming in four seasons, is the most impressive in this mountain, covering the whole mountain and shining like morning glow. This is the "Meihailing Park", the urban garden of Xiamen City on the Dongping Mountain. In the garden, over 10 thousand bougainvilleas of more than 50 varieties are planted.

　　Going across Meihailing Park, you will arrive at Dongping Mountain Water Reserve. Against the sparkling ripples, you can find the fishing people. The agritainment in the surrounded area and petty homestays in the mountains also attract many people to visit this scenic spot. People regard this place as the first choice of destination for relaxing and returning to nature probably because they can sit in the green shade and smell the sea breeze.

仙岳山

　　仙岳山位于厦门岛西北部，高212.7米，犹如镶嵌在城市中的绿宝石，郁郁葱葱，森林覆盖率达90%以上。作为全长23公里、串联八山三水的厦门山海健康步道中的一段，仙岳山步道一路绿意盎然，山花烂漫，美不胜收，更有全线唯一一座玻璃观景平台，可使人真正感受到立足"山海"之美。

　　这座开放式的山地公园内设"仙岳大观""琼华仙境""林海斜阳""翠峰揽月""天街餐霞""福寿洞天""松柏烟树""天竺岩寺"八大景区，是人们登山、锻炼、享受自然的好去处。

　　坐落在此的福德正神土地公庙作为仙岳山一道亮丽的人文景观，荟萃了国家级非物质文化遗产木雕、石雕、剪瓷雕等诸多闽南传统工艺，是目前全国最大的木结构土地公庙。

Xianyue Mountain

　　Xianyue Mountain is located in the northwest Xiamen Island with an altitude of 212.7 meters. It resembles the emerald in the city due to the fact that the percentage of forest coverage is over 90%. As a part of the 23-kilometer Xiamen Mountains-to-Sea Trail connecting eight mountains, two lakes and Wuyuan bay, the hiking trail in Xianyue Mountain is brimming over with exuberant green and blooming mountain flowers along the way, which is extremely attractive. Moreover, it possesses the only glass viewing deck in the whole trail, on which tourists can immerse themselves into the beauty of "mountain and sea".

　　Eight scenic spots are included in this open mountain park, including "Xianyue Grand View", "Qionghua Xianjing", "Linhai Xieyang", "Cuifeng Lanyue", "Tianjie Canxia", "Fushou Dongtian", "Songbai Yanshu" and "Tianzhuyan Temple", which serve as good destinations for people to climb up, exercise and enjoy the beauty of nature.

　　As a splendid human and cultural landscape located here, the Temple of Earth God built for Deity Fu De collects various traditional techniques of state-level intangible cultural heritage in southern Fujian, including sculpture of wood, stone and porcelain. Furthermore, it is the largest Earth God Temple made up of wood in China.

狐尾山

　　狐尾山位于厦门岛西部，紧邻海沧大桥，山体呈东北西南走向，由大小九个山峰组成，主峰海拔139.45米。层峦叠嶂的山峰、茂盛葱郁的林木、清幽浓郁的山林气息，对于日夜生活于繁华都市的人们来说，狐尾山无疑是迷你的森林氧吧。

　　顺着山间环形的步行道而上，沿途以自然地貌与植物景观取胜。在西部，"西峰览海"景区内，登高远眺，西海域尽收眼底；在南部，"南台城光"景区内，设有300平方米的观景平台，时常聚集着上山泡茶聊天的人们，抿口清茶，配些甜点，不觉月上树梢，远眺只见霓虹闪烁，高高低低的楼宇、环绕穿行的高架、车流如织的马路……城市画卷尽在眼前。

Huwei Mountain

　　Huwei Mountain is located in the western Xiamen Island and closely adjacent to Haicang Bridge, which is composed of nine peaks with the mountain ranging from northeast to southwest. The main peak is 139.45 meters high. For people who always live in the bustling cities, there is no doubt that Huwei Mountain is a mini forest oxygen bar for its range of peaks, lush forests, and the serene and intense breath of trees and forests.

　　Along the annular walking path in the mountain, the natural topography and plant landscape are among the best. In "Xifeng Lanhai (enjoying sea from the west peak)" scenic spot in the west, the entire west sea area is unfolded before your eyes if you stand at a high position. In "Nantai Chengguang (viewing the city from the southern platform)" in the south, a viewing platform of 300 square meters is established, where people gather together to enjoy tea and chat. They often sip a cup of tea together with some dessert. Unknowingly, it is getting late and only the shining neon lights, high and small buildings, surrounding viaducts and busy roads can be seen at a distance. The picture scroll of a city appears in front of your eyes.

天竺山

　　天竺山位于海沧区东孚街道，距厦门市区36公里，森林覆盖率达96.8%，山势磅礴，峰崖壮观，最高峰天柱山海拔933米。山上拥有森林植物200多种、野生动物40多种，自然资源丰富，景致迷人，四季各异。

　　奇岩怪石是天竺山的一大特色，仙桃石、海龟石、鹰嘴岩、巨石坊、八仙桌、千丈岩……引人无穷的遐思。在这绿色的世界里，天竺湖、两二湖、皓月湖等五个人工水库如五颗珍珠镶嵌在林海之中，清澈如镜。

Tianzhu Mountain

　　Tianzhu Mountain lies in the Dongfu Sub-district, Haicang District, 36 kilometres from the Xiamen city. The forest cover percentage is 96.8%. The mountain, peaks and cliffs are all very magnificent. The highest peak of Tianzhu Mountain has an altitude of 933 meters. The mountain owns rich natural resources with over 200 kinds of forest plants and over 40 kinds of wild animals. The scenery is extraordinary and each season has its advantages.

　　Strange rocks and bizarre stones are the important features of Tianzhu Mountain, such as Xiantao (Peach) Stone, Haigui (Turtle) Stone, Yingzui (Olecranon) Stone, Jushi Fang (Giant Stone Gateway), Baxian (the eight immortals in a Chinese legend) Table, Qianzhang (over 3 kilometers) Cliff and so on, which inspire infinite imaginations. In this green world, five artificial reservoirs, such as Tianzhu Lake, Liang'er Lake and Haoyue Lake, resemble five pearls installed into the sea of forests, which are as clean as mirrors.

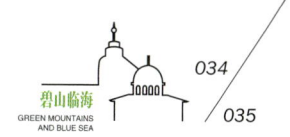

北辰山

北辰山位于同安城区东北12公里处,因"高拱北辰"得名,俗称北山。北辰山历史悠久,人杰地灵,同安历传"先有北山,后有同安"。北辰山为低山丘陵、花岗岩地貌,下游的竹坝水库水面宽阔,岸线曲折,在阳光的照射下犹如明镜。山顶水帘飞泻直下,山体被冲刷成一条峡谷和十二个大小不一的水潭,这便是北辰山著名的"十二龙潭",是厦门地区最大的瀑布景观。

除了秀丽的自然景观,北辰山亦有众多人文古迹。坐落在山麓的闽南古刹"广利庙",是五代时闽王王审知兄弟兵变开闽的肇始地。

Beichen Mountain

Beichen (the Polar Star) Mountain, 12 kilometers from the northeast of Tong'an District, gains its name from "as high as the Polar Star", and is often called Bei Mountain for short. Beichen Mountain has a long history and this rich land fosters many talents. It is recorded in the Tong'an history that "Bei Mountain emerged earlier than Tong'an". Beichen Mountain features low hills and granite geomorphology. The water of the Zhuba Reservoir downstream is wide and the coastline has twists and turns. It also shines like a mirror when exposed to the sun. The water curtain flows straight downward from the peak, and thus the mountain is washed into a canyon and twelve pools of different sizes, which are the famous "Twelve Dragon Ponds" of Beichen Mountain and the largest waterfall in Xiamen.

Apart from the pleasant natural scenery, Beichen Mountain also has many cultural relics. "Guangli Temple", the ancient temple located at the foot of the mountain in the southern Fujian, is where Wang Shenzhi, king of Min (the short name of Fujian) in the Five Dynasties, together with his brothers, led a mutiny and civilized Fujian which had been an isolated and poor place for a long time.

金光湖原始森林

　　初闻其名，不少人以为这是一片闪着金黄色光芒的湖泊，其实不然。

　　被誉为"闽南西双版纳"的金光湖原始森林位于同安区莲花镇内田村，因林区山形如湖状，有兔耳岭岩石之美，武夷山九曲之秀，四周六条山岭和两座小山交相环抱，构成"金"字形，旭日初生，叶露晶莹，金光闪闪，故得名"金光湖"。

　　这里古木参天，藤萝缠绕，林海茫茫，野草茵茵。景区拥有近5000亩原始森林，森林覆盖率达93%，林中含氧量和负离子数高于城市7倍，堪称少有的"天然氧吧"。

Jinguang Lake Old-growth Forest

　　On hearing the name for the first time, many people may think that it is a lake shining with the golden light. However, it is not the fact.

　　Jinguang (golden light) Lake Old-growth Forest, regarded as "Xishuangbanna in the southern part of Fujian province", is located in the Neitian Village, Lianhua Town, Tong'an District. It gains the name for several reasons: The shape of the mountain in the forests resembles a lake. And the beauty of Tu'erling Rock and streams of Jiuqu in Wuyi Mountain is among the best. Six ridges and two small mountains are interwoven together, resembling the character " 金 " in Chinese. Moreover, when the sun rises, the dewdrops on the leaves sparkle with golden glitter.

　　Here, the ancient trees tower into the sky; veins twist together; the forest sea and wild grass are vast. The scenic spot has nearly 5,000 mu (about 3.33 square kilometers) old-growth forest with a forest cover percentage of 93% and its forest oxygen content and negative ions are 7 times higher than the city. Therefore, it is a "natural oxygen bar" rare to be found.

香山

　　香山位于翔安区东南部，坐落于鸿渐山脉的南麓。"香山"原名"荒山"，南宋理学大师、时任同安县主簿朱熹曾数游此地，闻草木皆香，便将"荒山"更名为"香山"，有了理学大儒的赞语，香山千百年来声名远播。

　　"古寺古松古榕，民俗田园风光"，在周边吕塘民俗文化村以及众多景点的环绕中，东园村香山岩寺巍然坐落于山林之间，晨钟暮鼓，经声回荡。自然环境是香山的傲人之处，这里的空气清新，山青野绿，旅游资源丰富，又有村落星罗棋布，形成了古民居村落和梨园世家戏曲艺术学校相衬的独特人文景致。一年四季，鸟语花香，一望无垠的花海衬着连绵的青山，是繁忙的都市节奏中一隅灵魂的停留地。

Xiangshan Mountain

　　Xiangshan (fragrance) Mountain is located in the south of the Hongjian Mountain in the southeast of Xiang'an District. Xiangshan Mountain was originally known as "Huangshan (Barren) Mountain". Zhu Xi, the master of Neo-Confucianism and Zhubu (government official in charge of the clerical work) of the Tong'an County in the Southern Song Dynasty, travelled to this place for several times. Due to the fragrance of the plants, he changed the name from "Huangshan Mountain" to "Xiangshan Mountain". With the praise from the master of Neo-Confucianism, Xiangshan Mountain has been famous since then.

　　"The ancient temple with the ancient pines and banyans presents a luring scenery. The folk custom in this beautiful county attracts your attention." Surrounded by the Lvtang Folk Culture Village and many other scenic spots, the Xiangshanyan Temple of Dongyuan Village is located among the forests. The sounds of drum bell both in the morning and evening and sutra chanting echos in the valley. The Xiangshan Mountain is proud of its natural environment. The fresh air, green mountain, abundant tourism resources and the scattered villages form a unique landscape, with the ancient villages and the traditional Chinese opera school standing not far from each other. Throughout the whole year, a vast expanse of flowers decorates the green mountain along with the singing birds, and it is a haven for the busy souls from the city.

3 盎然
Vigorous

中山公园

  中山公园位于厦门老市区中心，始建于 1927 年，为纪念孙中山先生弘扬"天下为公"的精神而定名。公园利用当年的自然地形，依山就势，设东西南北四个各有特点的门楼。四门畅开，短墙通透，具有开放、外向的特色，与封闭、内向的中国传统园林迥异。

  公园南门东侧的醒狮球雕塑将醒狮、大鹏、地球仪结为一体——雕塑的球形表面镌刻着世界地图，球体下部环绕着四只展翅飞腾、锐眼利爪的大鹏，巧似雄鹰；球形顶部屹立着一头昂首怒吼的雄狮，寓意深邃，被誉为厦门第一城市雕塑，成为当时厦门的城标。

  时至今日，老厦门人口中所说的"公园"仍然特指中山公园，它是老厦门人心目中挥之不去的情结。

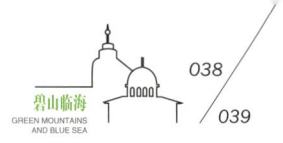

Zhongshan Park

Located in the center of the old town in Xiamen, Zhongshan Park was built in 1927 in order to commemorate Mr. Sun Yat-sen and promote the spirit of "The Whole World as One Community". Based on the original natural shape and geographical position, four gates with different characteristics were built in four directions at the background of mountains. With the gates open and the visibility of the low walls, the park commands a fine view, which is totally different from the closed and private traditional Chinese gardens.

In the east side of the South Gate, there is a statue of the Dancing Lion, which combines the dancing lion with the roc and tellurion. The surface of the ball is carved with the world map, and the bottom of the ball is surrounded by four flying rocs with sharp eyes and claws, which look just like eagles. On the top of the ball, there is a roaring lion, which has a deep meaning and was honored as the First City Sculpture at that time.

Today, the "park" mentioned by the old generation of Xiamen people is used to refer specifically to the "Zhongshan Park", which stands for a lingering nostalgia in their mind.

园林植物园

　　园林植物园位于厦门岛东南隅的万石山中，始建于 1960 年，是福建省第一个植物园，亦是鼓浪屿—万石山国家级重点风景名胜区的重要组成部分，享有"植物王国""植物博物馆"的美誉。植物园俗称"万石植物园"，其名源于园中遍布的嶙峋怪石。厦门旧有二十四景，在植物园范围内就占六景，即"万笏朝天""中岩玉笏""天界晓钟""太平石笑""紫云得路""高读琴洞"，涵盖山、洞、岩、寺等景观。

　　植物园内各类草木葳蕤，已引种、收集 7000 多种（含品种）植物，汇集了裸子植物区、棕榈植物区、沙生植物区、蔷薇园、花卉园、雨林世界等植物专类园，既有迷人的滨海植被，又有奇趣的异国情调，郁郁葱葱，绝不辜负"万石涵翠"之美名。1984 年，邓小平在南洋杉草坪内亲手植下一株大叶樟，为植物园增辉不少。

Botanical Garden

　　The Botanical Garden is located in Wanshi Mountain in the southeast of Xiamen Island, which was built in 1960. It is not only the first botanical garden in Fujian Province but also an important part of the Gulangyu Island-Wanshi Mountain National Scenic Spot, which has the reputation of the "Botanical Kingdom" and the "Botanical Museum". The Botanical Garden is also called "Wanshi Botanic Garden" due to the rugged rocks in the garden. There used to have twenty-four scenic spots in Xiamen. Six of them are in the Botanical Garden, including "Wan Hu Chao Tian", "Zhongyan Yu Hu", "The Tianjie Bell", "Tai Ping Shi Xiao", "Zi Yun De Lu" and "Gao Du Qin Dong". It covers mountains, caves, rocks, temples and so on.

　　There are many kinds of plants in the garden. Over kinds of 7,000 plants are planted, including gymnospermae garden, palm garden, desert plant garden, rose garden, flower garden, rainforest garden and so on. It has attracting coastal plants as well as exotic plants. "Wanshi Ever Green" is well known to the citizen. In 1984, Deng Xiaoping planted a deyenxial langedorffii in the araucaria lawn, which added great glory to the Botanical Garden.

白鹭洲公园

白鹭洲公园，是厦门最大的全开放式广场公园，位于市中心的筼筜湖上。白鹭洲毗邻市政府行政中心、滨北金融区及繁华老城区，优越的地理位置、良好的绿化景观与休闲文化设施使其成为厦门的城市"绿肺"，更是厦门的"城市客厅"。

公园主要以音乐喷泉广场为主题，以白鹭女神像和鸽子广场为中心。白鹭女神雕塑高13.6米，身姿优美，娴静地跪坐在一块巨岩上梳理长发，肩上停着一只小白鹭，是厦门的标志性雕塑。雕像前的广场上有广场鸽，与孩童亲近嬉戏，自由自在，好不热闹！

Bailuzhou Park

Bailuzhou Park is the largest fully open square park in Xiamen, located in Yundang Lake of the city's center. Bailuzhou is next to the government's administration center, the financial areas of Binbei and the bustling old town. Due to the excellent geographical location, beautiful green landscape and entertainment facilities, Bailuzhou becomes the "Green Lung" and even the "City Livingroom" of Xiamen.

The park takes the Music Fountain Square as its theme and Bailu Goddess as well as Pigeon Square as its center. The statue of Bailu Goddess is 13.6 meters high. It is kneeling on a rock while combing her hair, and there has a Bailu (egret) on her shoulder, which is an iconic sculpture in Xiamen. There are pigeons flying around the square in front of the statue, and children can play with them. What a free and happy moment!

南湖公园

　　南湖公园位于筼筜湖东南岸，始建于 1989 年，1995 年 1 月建成开放，面积 16 万平方米，湖面 2.86 万平方米，是一座颇具现代风格的市级综合性公园。

　　公园内有"筼筜春晓""曲岸荷香""四宜书院""坐石临流""茗香园"等景点。"筼筜春晓"以水榭码头为主景，密林前满是如怒火般盛开的木棉与象牙红，配以疏林草地，湖岸点缀垂柳，形成一幅春花烂漫的景象；"坐石临流"由人工叠石、假山、小瀑布组成，游人穿石钻洞、越水跳润，趣从中来。

Nanhu Park

　　Covering 160,000 square meters and opened in January 1995, Nanhu Park is in the southeast bank of the Yundang Lake, built in 1989. The lake covers an area of 28,600 square meters. Nanhu Park is a municipal park with modern style and comprehensive functions.

　　There are "Yundang Chun Xiao", "Qu An He Xiang", "Si Yi Shu Yuan", "Zuo Shi Lin Liu", "Ming Xiang Yuan" and other scenic spots. The "Yundang Chun Xiao" has a wharf as the main spot. With the blooming kapok and coral erythrina as well as the grass and willows, it presents a scenery full of flowers and spring atmosphere. "Zuo Shi Lin Liu" consists of artificial stones, rockery and small waterfalls. The tourists can cross through the cave and jump among the stones. It is extremely interesting.

铁路文化公园

轨道上斑驳的锈迹，扑面而来的原始气息，这里，曾经是火车风驰电掣般驶过的老铁路。

东起金榜公园，西至和平码头，铁路文化公园全长约4.5公里，宽12到18米，沿线串联起金榜公园、园林植物园、虎溪岩、鸿山公园等景区，是一个独特而具有历史内涵的带状公园。

"铁路"二字，恰道出这座公园的特色——昔日，那长长的铁轨如同一条蜿蜒的小河通向远方。20世纪80年代开始，此线路闲置，却保留了厦门交通发展的最初记忆。如今，旧铁路被打造成赏心悦"木"、品味厦门的城市新名片。古老而浪漫的铁道情结，文化味儿十足。

Railway Culture Park

The mottled rust on the track along with the original feelings tells the tourists that there used to be an old railway with train running through.

Starting from the east of Jinbang Park to the west of Heping Wharf, the Railway Culture Park is 4.5 kilometers long and 12–18 meters wide. Jinbang Park, Botanical Garden, Huxi Rock, Hongshan Park and other scenic spots are connected in a line. It is a park with a particular historical meaning.

"Railway" reflects the characteristics of this park. In the old days, the long railway ran far away just like the river. Since the 1980s, the railway has not been used any more. However, it has still retained the initial memory of Xiamen's traffic development. Now, the old track becomes a new "namecard" for Xiamen. The old but romantic track is full of cultural atmosphere.

五缘湾湿地公园

水在脚边流,花在身边开,人在画中行——五缘湾湿地公园是"隐藏"在城市里的"世外桃源",是五缘湾与湖边水库有机连接形成的厦门岛内唯一咸、淡水交界地。公园占地89公顷,面积相当于半个鼓浪屿,是厦门最大的湿地生态园区,被誉为厦门的"绿肺"。

公园设有湿地生态自然保护区、红树林植物区、鸟类观赏区、环湖休闲运动区等,拥有上百种各类野生植物及数十种珍稀鸟类。其中"黑天鹅天堂"有数百只黑天鹅优雅地游弋湖面,翩翩起舞,勾勒出一幅美丽的图画。

碧山临海
GREEN MOUNTAINS
AND BLUE SEA

044 / 045

Wuyuan Bay Wetland Park

With the river running through your feet and flowers blooming in front of your eyes, you feel just like you are inside the picture. Wuyuan Bay Wetland Park is a hidden haven in the city. It is the place where Wuyuan Bay is organically connected with the Hubian Reservoir where the salt water and the fresh water meet. Covering an area of 89 hectares, it is the half size of Gulangyu Island and the largest wetland ecological park in Xiamen. It is also called the "Green lung" of Xiamen.

There are wetland ecological reserve, mangrove plant area, bird ornamental area, leisure sports areas and so on in the park. There are also over one hundred wild plants and dozens of birds which can rarely be seen, including the black swan dancing in the water, which makes a beautiful picture.

五通灯塔公园

　　灯塔指引方向，寓意希望与未来。位于厦门岛最东部的五通灯塔就是这样一座充满朝气的地标性建筑。这座伟岸灯塔的实际功用为翔安海底隧道的通风出气口，经过设计者的巧妙构思，它被建成一座灯塔，沐浴晨光，分外妖娆，是厦门最佳观日处。

　　走进公园，一座圆柱状的红顶灯塔高高矗立，塔身上"五通灯塔"四个红色大字映入眼帘。沿着笔直的灯塔大道向前走，30座精美的灯塔雕塑台分布于道路两侧，每座雕塑台都用影雕的形式介绍一座世界知名的灯塔，并刻有其名称、所在的国家、高度以及建设缘由；灯塔基座平台上镌刻了10幅浮雕，分别展现世界上最著名的10座海上灯塔，打造出别具一格的灯塔文化。

Wutong Lighthouse Park

　　Lighthouse guides the direction, implying hope and future. Located in the east of Xiamen, Wutong Lighthouse is such a vibrant landmark. This splendid lighthouse is actually used for ventilation for the Xiang'an Subsea Tunnel. Through the elaborate and ingenious design, it is built in the form of a lighthouse, which looks more enchanting under the sun. And it is the best place to watch the sunrise and sunset.

　　Entering the park, you could see that a red cylindrical lighthouse stands tall. Four red Chinese characters "Wutong Lighthouse" on the tower are in sight. Going straight along the road, 30 beautiful lighthouse sculptures are located on both sides of the road. Each sculpture introduces a world famous lighthouse in the form of stone-shadow carving, engraved with its name, country, height and construction reasons; on the platform of the lighthouse, 10 reliefs are carved, showing 10 of the world's most famous lighthouses, which creates a unique lighthouse culture.

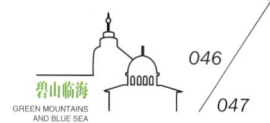

忠仑公园

　　忠仑公园原为忠仑苗圃,位于厦门岛东部,北连湖边水库,南接东芳山别墅区,东邻蔡塘社区,西毗金尚路。公园总面积约65万平方米,其中约37万平方米是长满参天大树的风景林地。"云顶岩—忠仑公园—湖边水库"观景轴线犹如一条绿色的长廊,镶嵌在城市中,成为厦门岛的第二个筼筜湖生态景区,忠仑公园恰处于中心位置。

　　园内的东芳山植被茂密,有相思林、龙眼林、柠檬林,形态各异的石头遍布,是登高览胜、休闲放松的好去处。每年阳春三月,清风和煦,桃花正艳,忠仑公园总会迎来大批赏花的游人,漫步花间,缕缕馨香沁人心脾,漫山遍野的粉嫩桃红中尽是人们绽放的笑颜。

Zhonglun Park

　　Zhonglun Park was originally the Zhonglun Nursery Garden. It is located in the east of Xiamen Island, and it lies to the south of the Hubian Reservoir, north of Dongfang Mountain villas, west of Caitang Community, and east of Jinshang Road. The total area of the park is about 650 thousand square meters, of which about 370 thousand square meters are scenic woodlands with towering trees. From Yunding Rock to Zhonglun Park and to the Hubian Reservoir, the viewing axis is like a green corridor embedded in the city. It becomes the second Yundang Lake Ecological Scenic Spot of Xiamen Island, and Zhonglun Park is at the center area.

　　Dongfang Mountain in the park is a dense forest, including Acacia Forest, Longyan Forest, Lemon Grove as well as different forms of stones, which is a wonderful place to relax and go climbing. Every March, the breeze is warm and the peach blossom is gorgeous. A large number of visitors come to Zhonglun Park to admire the beauty of flowers and walk among the flowers where fragrance refreshes their minds. Among the delicate pink all over the mountain, this place is brimmed with visitors' smiles.

海湾公园

　　海湾公园占地面积约 20 万平方米,地势平坦,东邻筼筜湖与白鹭洲公园,西临西海湾,可远眺海沧新城;西北方向横卧着海沧大桥,视线之内还有氤氲中若隐若现的鼓浪屿,美景尽收眼底。

　　公园分为天园、地园、林园、草园、水花园、滨海风光和星光大道等七大景区,以星光大道为界,分为北园和南园。远远望去,海湾公园如一缕翠绿色的缎带,将大海与筼筜湖温柔地系在一起,湖海相接,海天相连。

　　沿着海湾公园堤岸一直到海边的木栈道,这里是别具风味的露天酒吧一条街。夜幕降临之际,伴着微咸的海风,与三五好友喝酒畅聊,伴着驻唱歌手酣畅淋漓的歌声与台下此起彼伏的欢呼声,醉饮无敌海景,好不痛快!

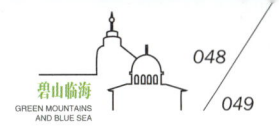

Haiwan Park

Haiwan Park covers an area of about 200 thousand square meters, wide and flat. It lies to Yundang Lake and Bailuzhou Park in the east, and Western Sea Bay in the west, overlooking the Haicang Xincheng. In the northwest, there lies the Haicang Bridge, and Gulangyu Island is partly hidden and partly visible, where panoramic view of the beautiful scenery is in sight.

The park is divided into seven scenic spots, including Tian Yuan, Di Yuan, Lin Yuan, Cao Yuan, Shuihua Yuan, Seaside Scenery and Avenue of Stars. With the Avenue of Stars as the boundary, they can be divided into the North Park and South Park. Looking from afar, the Haiwan Park is like a green ribbon connecting the sea with the Yundang Lake gently together, while the great sea stretches away to meet the sky.

Along the embankment of Haiwan Park to the wooden boardwalk along the coast, there is a special open-air bar street. When night falls, with the salty sea breeze, we can chat and drink with several friends, listening to the singer singing and the audiences cheering. How wonderful the seascape is! What a delight!

园林博览苑

　　园林博览苑建在杏林湾上，是世界独一无二的"水上大观园"，这里举办过2007年第六届中国（厦门）国际园林花卉博览会。其最大特色即"海上建园"，经过清淤吹沙充填，从区域外补充350多万立方米沙壤土、田园种植土进行人工造地。

　　园区旅游资源丰富，拥有九座特色风光岛、百个地域史实园林、舒适惬意的海水温泉以及标志景观杏林阁与月光环。这里九岛棋布，百园争艳，景观优美，生态和谐，拥有多岛环绕、众星拱月的"园在水上、水在园中"的独特景观，可谓"虽为人作，宛如天开"，是厦门这座"海上花园"一张重要的城市名片。

Xiamen Horticulture Expo Garden

　　The Xiamen Horticulture Expo Garden is built in the Xinglin Bay, which is an unparalleled "water garden" around the world. The Sixth China (Xiamen) International Garden & Flower Expo was held here in 2007. Its biggest feature is the "sea garden". After dredging and sand filling, the land is artificially constructed by some 3.5 million cubic meters of sandy soils and garden planting soils from outside areas.

　　The park is rich in tourism resources. It enjoys splendid scenic spots, including nine special scenery islands, hundred historical gardens, comfortable seawater hot spring, landmark Xinglin Pavilion and Moonlight Ring. Here, nine islands spread all over, and gardens are full of vibrance, with beautiful landscape and a harmonious ecological system. It boasts the unique landscape of "garden in the water, water in the garden" surrounded by islands, which is why people say "although it is made by man, it seems to be created by the nature". That is a significant city name card of Xiamen, a "garden on the sea".

THREE

人文印记
CULTURAL IMPRESSIONS

厦门，这里镌满**人文印记**，人杰痕迹在**讨海**与**信俗**中世代巧琢。

Abundant with celebrities and cultural relics, Xiamen has been enriched through fish trade and local customs generation after generation.

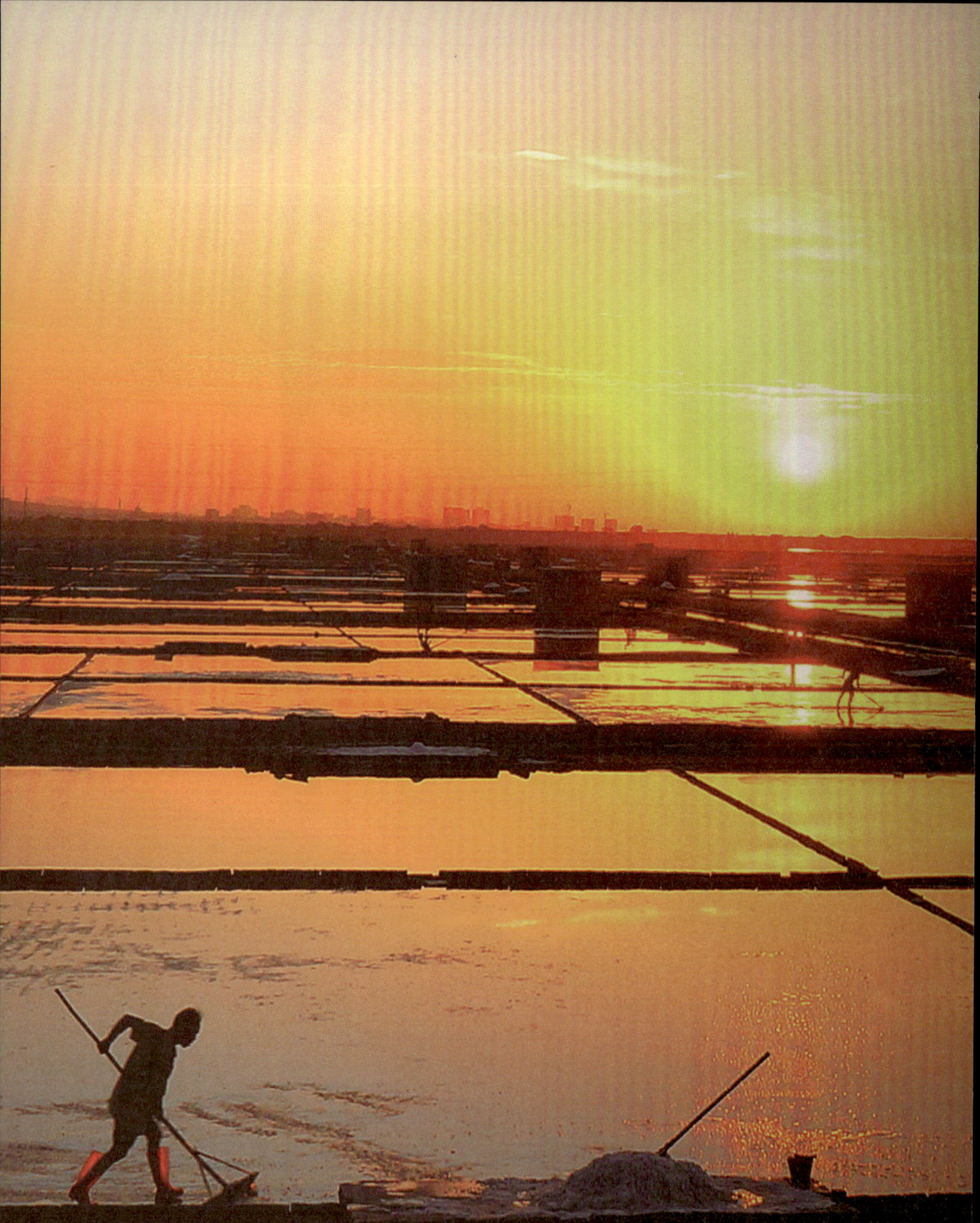

土耳其诗人纳乔姆·希格梅说:"人的一生中有两样东西是永远不会忘记的,那就是母亲的面孔和城市的面貌。"

厦门的美,有自然之美,更有人文之美。

厦门的文化气息,邂逅在不经意的角落里。站在现代化的摩天大楼顶上,鹭江街道一带老街旧厝尽收眼底,逼仄小巷、沧桑骑楼、深深老宅、红砖古厝。五老峰传来古刹钟声,起落的潮水,轻轻拍打在沙坡尾的岸边,市井味十足的老厦门在时光中悠转,这就是厦门的"乡愁"。

宋代大儒朱熹在此建立经史阁,留下一处处墨宝遗迹;民族英雄郑成功在此操练水师,从这里出发,收复了被荷兰殖民者侵占多年的台湾;华侨领袖陈嘉庚在昔日偏僻的渔村里建设起举世闻名的现代学校;当代诗人舒婷在这里悠然行走,浪漫赋诗……

厦门是文化荟萃之地,有着与众不同的城市性格、独一无二的城市特色、吸引眼球的城市魅力、丰富多彩的闽南文化,以优雅进取的市民精神,谱写着闽南神韵最新篇章。

"There are two things that one can forget only in death, the face of one's mother and the face of one's hometown," said the Turkish poet Nazim Hikmet.

Xiamen's beauty not only lies in the nature, but also lies in its people and culture.

Wherever you are, you may find yourself embraced by the cultural atmosphere of Xiamen. Standing at the top of the modern skyscrapers, you can have a bird view of Lujiang Ave, the panoramic view of the old house on this old street, and the view of the cramming alleys, weather-beaten arcades, the old houses, and the ancient houses with red bricks. The bell from the temples of Wulao Peaks, the ups and downs of the tide which gently taps on the shores, and the old Xiamen full of vitality which experienced a long history all constitute the "nostalgia" of Xiamen.

In the Song Dynasty, Zhu Xi, the master of Neo-Confucianism, built historical pavilions here, leaving literary masterpieces. Zheng Chenggong, the national hero trained the navy here, and started from here to reclaim Taiwan which had been colonized by Dutch for several years. Tan Kah Kee, the leader of the overseas Chinese, established a world's well-known modern school in a remote fishing village. Shu Ting, the modern poet, leisurely walked around the city and wrote romantic poems.

Xiamen enjoys splendid culture, with distinct city characteristics, unique city style, attractive city charm, and various South Fujian cultures. It writes the latest chapter of South Fujian with its elegant and enterprising spirit.

1 巧琢 Exquisite Carving

骑楼

就像北京宽绰疏朗的四合院，上海中西合璧的石库门一样，骑楼，是厦门传统文化的符号。

骑楼出现，不过百年，但它在短短时间里风靡闽南，成为主要街景。

骑楼建筑的盛行，20世纪初的"下南洋"热潮功不可没。许多在异乡发达的归国华侨，为家乡带回新的商业理念，带回风情别致的南洋建筑。骑楼这种"商住合一"的居所应运而生，最早出现在中山路、大生里。

骑楼上楼下廊，上面是住家，下面是店铺，既扩大了居住面积，又变成与顾客的共享空间；既可以遮风挡雨，让顾客倍感舒适，又拥有精致考究的店面，显示出店主与众不同的品位。

与鼓浪屿遥遥相望的鹭江道沿线骑楼建筑已有百年历史，是厦门一道独特的风景线。

人文印记
CULTURAL IMPRESSIONS

054 / 055

Arcade Building

Just like the broad quadrangle courtyard in Beijing, and the Shikumen with Chinese and western features in Shanghai, the arcade building is the symbol of Xiamen's traditional culture.

Arcade building just exists for more than one hundred years. However, during this short period of time, it has become popular in South Fujian as an important landscape on the street.

The popularity of arcade buildings is due to the boom of "going overseas" at the beginning of the 20th century. Many overseas Chinese who made a great fortune in foreign countries came back home with new business ideas as well as unique foreign architectures. Therefore, arcade building which can be used to "live and do business" came into being. It was early built on Zhongshan Rd and Dashengli.

Within the arcade building, the upstairs has rooms where people live while the downstairs has corridors which are used as shops. This not only enlarges the living space, but also creates a new shared space for customers. It can not only provide shelters but also make customers feel comfortable. In addition, it has exquisite stores and shows the different tastes of life of the owners at the same time.

The arcade buildings along Lujiang Ave, which are on the opposite of Gulangyu Island enjoy a history of more than 100 years. They can be regarded as a unique feature of Xiamen.

鼓浪屿万国建筑

岁月的风霜增添了鼓浪屿的历史厚度。

19世纪中叶,厦门开放为通商口岸。鼓浪屿因自然条件优越而成为在厦外国人首选的办公地和居住地。先后有13个国家在鼓浪屿设立领事馆,英、美、法等国侨民在此兴建教堂,开办学校、医院及洋行。20世纪上半叶,富商、华侨也纷纷到鼓浪屿建宅置业,兴建了大量的西式或中西合璧式的私家宅院。现今,岛上所存19世纪末至20世纪上半叶建造的各式建筑共1000余座,其建筑形式多样,建筑质量上乘,鼓浪屿因此被誉为"万国建筑的汇集地"。

这些建筑小巧玲珑,散落在山坡、海边的绿树丛中,幽静别致,许多建筑有浓烈的欧陆风格。中国园林建筑的廊、亭、阁、楼、桥样式齐全,古希腊的陶立克、爱奥尼克、科林斯三大柱式各展其姿,罗马式的圆柱,哥特式的尖顶,伊斯兰式的圆顶,巴洛克式的浮雕,门楼壁炉、阳台、钩栏、凸拱窗,争相斗妍,异彩纷呈,洋溢着古典主义和浪漫主义的色彩,构成鼓浪屿中西文化交流的精粹景观。

2017年7月8日,"鼓浪屿历史国际社区"成功列入"世界文化遗产"名录。

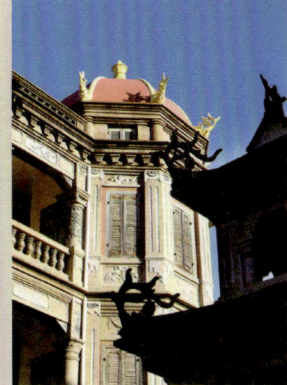

World Architecture in Gulangyu Island

As the time goes by, all vicissitudes add the historical depth of Gulangyu Island.

In the middle of the 19th century, Xiamen was opened as a trading port. With advantageous natural conditions, Gulangyu Island became the first office and living place for foreigners in Xiamen. There were successively 13 countries establishing consulates on Gulangyu Island, and countries like Britain, America and France set up churches, schools, hospitals and foreign banks here. In the first half of the 20th century, wealthy businessmen and overseas Chinese bought houses and started their careers here, and thus large numbers of private houses which were in western style or in both western and Chinese styles were built. Up till now, there are over 1000 kinds of architectures that were built from the end of the 19th century to the first half of the 20th century, with various building types and high quality. Therefore, Gulangyu Island was regarded as the "gathering place of world's architecture".

Small and sophisticated, these architectures are distributed among the forests on the mountains or along the seaside. Located in the quiet environment, many of these architectures are in a strong European style. There are corridors, pavilions, buildings and bridges in the Chinese garden style, three columns of the Doric, Ionic and Corinthian style in ancient Greek, Romanesque columns, Gothic spires, Islamic domes, Baroque reliefs, as well as doorway fireplaces, balconies, balustrades, and arched windows. All these are shining with beauty and colors on this island. The classicism and romanticism reflected by these architectures stand for the exchange between Chinese and western cultures on Gulangyu Island.

On July 8, 2017, "Gulangyu Historical International Community" was successfully included into the World Heritage list.

嘉庚建筑

　　著名华侨领袖陈嘉庚先生倾资办学，在家乡厦门投资创立并亲自规划建设了著名的集美学校和厦门大学，建成了一批具有独特风格的中西合璧的"嘉庚建筑"。

　　嘉庚建筑具有统一而鲜明的风格，空间结构注重与环境相协调，将闽南屋顶特色与西式屋身巧妙糅合，形成闽南古民居"飞檐翘脊"屋顶和西洋"白墙石柱"屋身结构，拼花、细作、线脚则具有闽南或南洋风格，被厦门人生动地形容为"头戴斗笠、身穿西装"。厦门大学的群贤楼群、建南楼群，集美学校的南熏楼、延平楼、尚忠楼均是嘉庚风格建筑的典型代表。

　　这种建筑样式体现特定历史时代的风貌，历经半个多世纪的沧桑，依然优雅从容，散发着成熟的魅力。

Architectures with Jiageng Style

　　Chen Jiageng, also known as Tan Kah Kee, the famous leader of overseas Chinese, invested a large sum of money to establish schools in his hometown, Xiamen. He established and planned two famous school campuses by himself, namely Jimei School and Xiamen University, which have become a group of unique "architecture with Jiageng style" combining the Chinese and western building features.

　　Architectures with Jiageng style have unified and distinct features, focusing on the coordination between the space structure and the environment. They integrate the unique features of the roof in South Fujian and the main part of the western houses, forming the structures including roofs with "cornices and ridges" of ancient dwellings and main parts of "white walls and stone columns". The pattern, exquisite building and molding of them are all in the style of South Fujian or Southeast Asia. They are vividly described by Xiamen people as men "wearing a bamboo hat and a business suit". The Qunxian Building Complex, Jiannan Builidng Complex in Xiamen University, and the Nanxun Building, Yanping Building, Shangzhong Building in Jimei School are all typical architectures with Jiageng style.

　　This kind of architecture reflects certain historical appearance of a time. After experiencing vicissitudes of more than a half century, these architectures are still elegant and attractive.

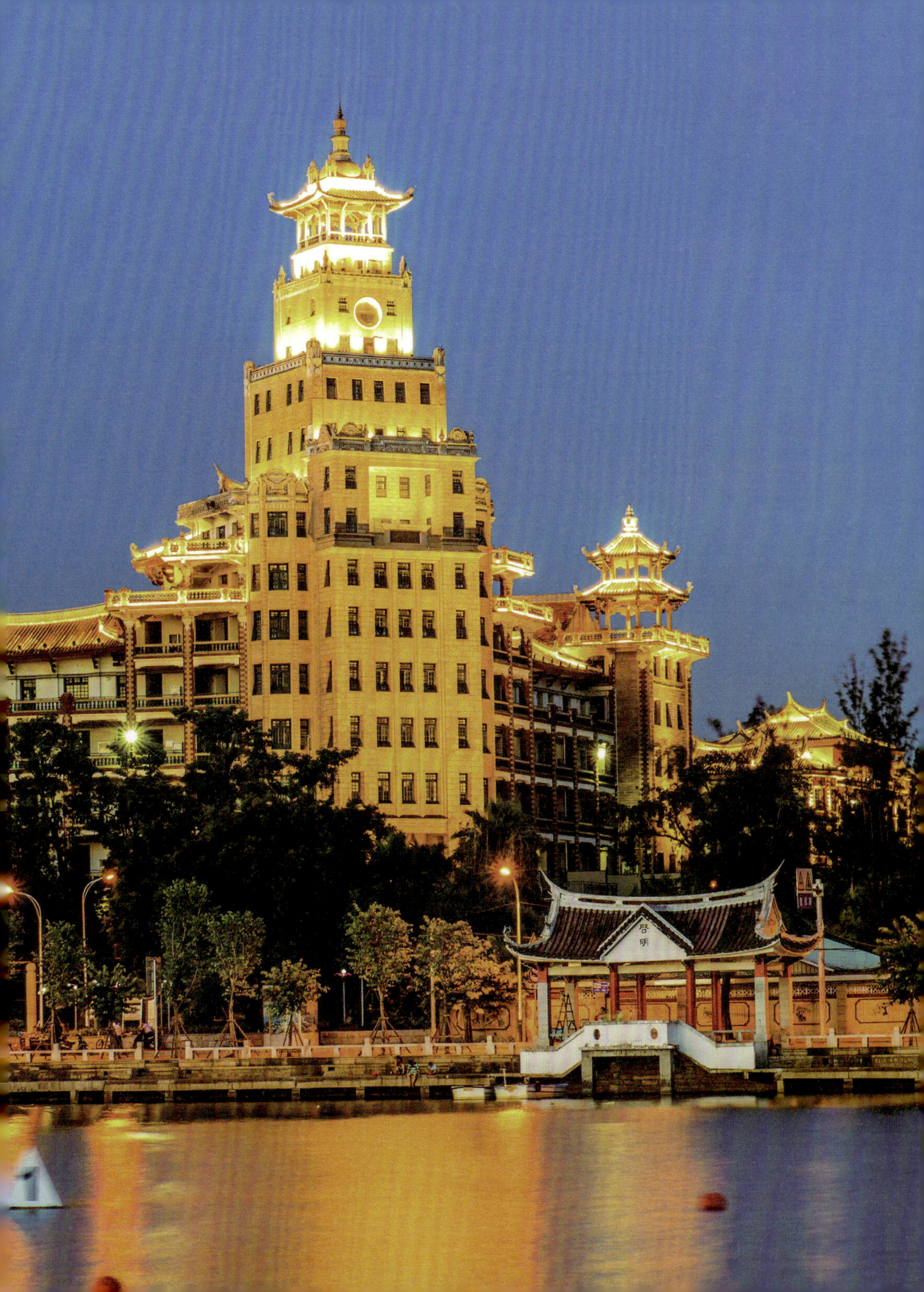

红砖古厝

闽南地区盛产高品质的红土,用红土烧制出的红砖、红瓦被闽南人用作建造房屋的重要材料。

红砖古厝具有整体形式美,丰富变化的砖石墙面,讲究细节的可视性和图像故事的可读性,图案附载象征隐喻。由于地理和历史的缘故,厦门的红砖古厝也带有浓厚的海洋气息。

它是真正代表厦门历史文化的地上文物,它们或静静地藏在老市区里青石板的小巷中,或散落在厦门的乡间原野上,红砖为墙,红瓦为顶,在蓝天下展示着浓郁的地域特色。

坐落于繁华中山路段的兰琴古厝,高堂大瓦,水榭歌台,曲径幽通,庭院深深,系厦门现今保存最完整的典型闽南风格古建筑。在厝中盘桓小憩,恍若阳春召烟景。

位于海沧的莲塘别墅,冠绝八闽大地,最能彰显红砖古厝特色,住宅、学堂、家庙三者呈"品"字形分布,是厦门目前保存面积最大的古建筑群,兼具人居、教育、祭祀三重功能。

Ancient Houses with Red Bricks

　　South Fujian has rich high-quality red clay, which can be used to fire red bricks and red tiles as important materials to build houses.

　　Ancient houses with red bricks are beautiful in the whole sense, with various brick walls, detailed visuality, and readable image stories. The images on the wall have metaphorical meanings. Due to the geographical and historical reasons, ancient houses with red bricks in Xiamen also have strong maritime flavor.

　　This is the real aboveground cultural relic that represents the culture and history of Xiamen. Lying quietly on the small streets in the old city center, or on the fields in rural areas of Xiamen, these walls of red bricks and roofs of red tiles demonstrate the strong local features of Xiamen.

　　Located at the bustling Zhongshan Road, Lanqin Ancient House has high halls, large tiles and waterside pavilions which are quiet and deep. It is the ancient building of the typical South Fujian style that is most completely preserved. You can have a rest in the house, and enjoy the sunshine and the beautiful views outside the window.

　　Liantang Villa, located in Haicang, is quite outstanding among all the other architectures in Fujian. It best represents the layout of the Chinese character " 品 " typically found in old houses with red bricks, including the living houses, schools, and family temples. It is now the largest ancient architecture group well preserved in Xiamen, which has three major functions of dwelling, education and fete.

2 讨海
Living on the Sea

第八市场

　　第八市场位于近代厦门市政建设的第一条马路——开元路边上，紧靠第一、二码头，是厦门最有名的海鲜市场。从前龙溪、海澄的渔民讨小海，都将海产品运到这里售卖，早市或晚市，视潮水而定。

　　八市的海产品不仅数量多于一般的农贸市场，种类也尤其繁多。卖海鲜的摊贩满满当当地排列在街面上和骑楼下，地摊上摆满马鲛鱼、黄翅鱼、黄花鱼、巴浪鱼、螃蟹……琳琅满目。

　　近百年来，八市一直受到新老厦门人和许多外地游客的喜爱，他们把到八市闲逛当作深入最真实的本地民间生活、了解最真切的老厦门的途径。

The Eighth Market

The Eighth Market is located on Kaiyuan Rd, the first road built in the urban construction of modern Xiamen, close to the First Wharf and the Second Wharf. It is the most famous seafood market in Xiamen. In the past, the fishermen in Longxi Town and Haideng Town often went on a small expedition, which means they often sell seafood here. Whether they would sell on the morning market or the evening market depends on the tide.

The number of seafood sold on the Eighth Market is larger than other markets, and the options are more. The vendors that sell seafood are full of the street and under the arcade buildings. On the stalls, there are mackerel, yellow-winged fish, croaker, Japanese scad, crab and so on, which will dazzle your eyes.

Over the past one hundred years, the Eighth Market has always been popular among both the old and the new Xiamen people as well as many foreign tourists. They take wandering around the Eighth Market as the way to experience the most authentic local life and to understand the real old Xiamen.

曾厝垵

曾厝垵位于环岛路，本是一个靠海的小渔村。靠山吃山，靠水吃水，海边的人们世代讨海而生。男人们外出捕鱼，女人们在家耕种和操持家务。慢慢地，一幢一幢红砖翘角的闽南古厝依地势而立，渐渐形成一条条小巷。

如今，曾厝垵经过改造提升，变身为文艺聚集地，以其独特的地理优势和文艺气质，吸引来一群有才有创意的文艺青年驻扎，经营着令人着迷的梦幻店铺，让这个昔日小渔村变成今日名副其实的文创园。

Zengcuoan

Located at the Island Ring Blvd, Zengcuoan used to be a small fishing village near the sea. People who live by the mountain or the water would make their livings on the mountain or water. Therefore, people who live by the sea would make the living on the sea. Men always go fishing on the sea while women tend to farm or do housework at home. Gradually, many ancient houses with red bricks were established one after another and small alleys came into being.

Nowadays, after several changes and transformations, Zengcuoan has become the gathering place of literature and art. With its unique geographical advantage and artistic characteristic, Zengcuoan attracts many innovative artists to live here. They operate fascinating shops here, which turns this small fishing village to be a real cultural and recreational park.

沙坡尾

　　因为金黄金黄的沙滩，因为月牙般弯弯的港湾，沙坡尾早年的名字叫"玉沙坡"。

　　1684年，清政府在厦门设立闽海关，厦门港从此成为我国对外交通贸易的四大港之一。此后的一百年间，两岸贸易必须通过厦门来实现，厦门是大陆与台湾对渡的唯一港口，而渡口就在玉沙坡，也就是现在的沙坡尾。

　　渔民、船坞、矮房，隐于闹市的沙坡尾维系着老厦门的光景。被岁月洗礼过的石板路，带着锈迹斑斑的码头，见证了几代厦门人的成长。

　　老厦门的味道，成了文艺青年喜欢沙坡尾的理由。这里原先遍布着许多中小码头，如今已成为一个寻找美食和美店的绝佳去处。

Shapowei

　　Because of the golden beach and the crescent gulf, Shapowei used to be called "Yushapo (Jelly Sand Slope)".

　　In 1684, the Qing government set up the Fujian custom in Xiamen and thus Xiamen became one of the four biggest ports for foreign exchanges in China. For the next one hundred years, the trade exchange between both sides of the Taiwan Strait had to pass through Xiamen. Xiamen became the only port for the Chinese mainland and Taiwan to exchange goods, while the ferry was exactly at Yushapo, which is today's Shapowei.

　　Hidden in the downtown, with docks and low houses, Shapowei entails the scene of the old Xiamen. The stone road baptized by the time and the rusty wharf both witness the growth of several generations of Xiamen people.

　　The flavor of old Xiamen has become the reason why young people with artistic talents like to go to Shapowei. In the past, there were many small and medium-sized wharfs, but now it is a destination for delicious food and beautiful shops.

澳头村

　　澳头，位于翔安区新店镇，襟山带海，隔海与金厦两岛相望，既是闽南的著名侨乡，也是美丽的海港渔村。

　　澳头曾是闽南著名的古渡口，建有各类商铺和古街道，商贾云集，市井繁华。据史料记载，清道光元年（1821年），有澳头人驾驶的帆船经厦门港直达新加坡，这是我国直通新加坡的第一艘货船，也是新加坡开埠的第一条商船。从此，澳头人陆续出洋开荒拓土，目前，澳头人遍布世界14个国家和地区。

　　偎依着大海，港阔水深，澳头的每个角落洋溢着大海的气息。当夜幕降临时，渔船就像一颗颗璀璨的星星，点缀着无边无际的大海，渔民唱着幸福的歌谣，缓缓地驶回港湾，画面犹如一幅海天长卷，美轮美奂。

Aotou Village

　　Aotou Village, located in the Xindian Town in Xiang'an District, is near the sea and mountain. It is opposite to Kinmen Island and Xiamen Island across the sea. It is not only a famous hometown of overseas Chinese in South Fujian, but also a beautiful harbor and fishing village.

　　Aotou Village was once the famous ancient ferry in South Fujian, with all kinds of shops and old streets. There were many businessmen gathering here, forming a prosperous picture. According to historical materials, in 1821 (the first year of Daoguang of the Qing Dynasty), there was an Aotou person who drove a sailboat passing by Xiamen port to Singapore. This was the first cargo boat to arrive directly at Singapore from China, and was the first business boat to arrive at Singapore after it was open as a trading port. Since then, Aotou people began exploring other areas in foreign countries. Today, the footprints of Aotou people has covered more than 14 countries and regions in the world.

　　Due to the location near the sea and deep water within the port, every corner of Aotou Village has a flavor of the sea. Every time when the night falls, the fishing boats are like shiny stars in the sky, decorating the broad ocean. The fishermen sing happy songs, driving back to the ports. The scene is like a beautiful picture.

3 痕迹
Postwar Relics

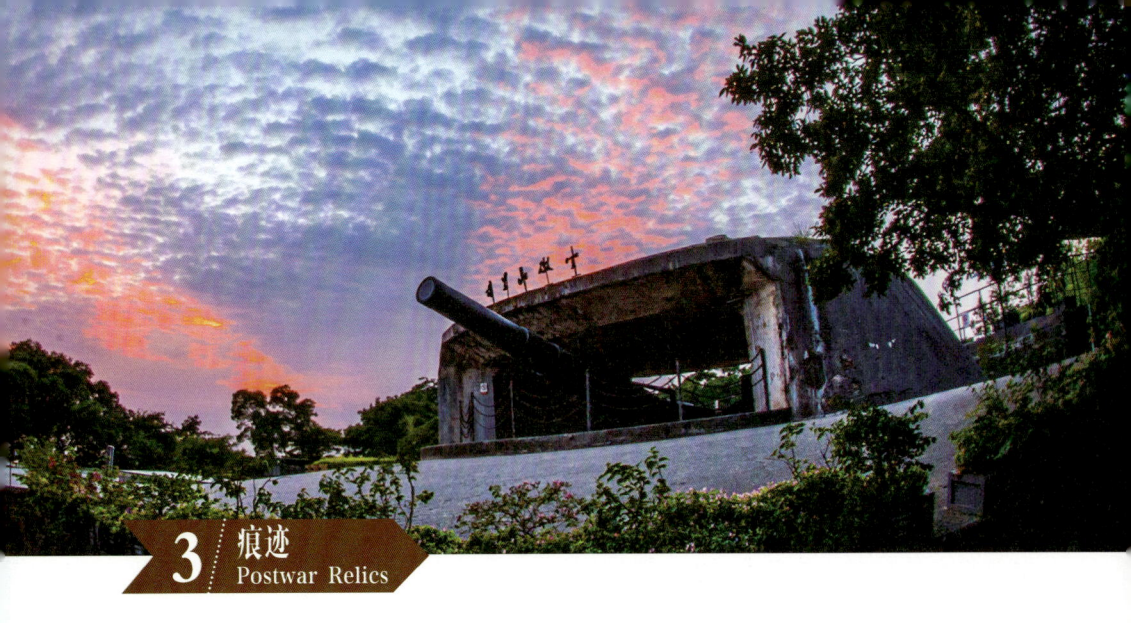

胡里山炮台

　　胡里山炮台位于厦门岛东南端海岬突出部，毗邻厦门大学，是洋务运动的产物，始建于清光绪二十年（1894年）三月初八，竣工于清光绪二十二年（1896年）十一月初八，号称"八闽门户天南锁钥"。

　　胡里山炮台上最有名的是清光绪十九年（1893年）购自德国克虏伯兵工厂的一门28生（280毫米）克虏伯大炮，至今保存完好，有效射程可达16000米（最远射程19760米），曾被鉴定为"世界现存原址上最古老最大的19世纪海岸炮"。

Hulishan Fortress

　　Located at the southeastern end of Xiamen, Hulishan Fortress is next to Xiamen University. As the product of Self-Strengthening Movement, it was built from March 8, 1894, the 20th year of Guangxu of the Qing Dynasty and finished on November 8, 1896, the 22nd year of Guangxu of the Qing Dynasty. It was regarded as "the key to the doors in Xiamen".

　　On the Hulishan Fortress, the most famous cannon is the 280 mm Krupp cannon bought from German Krupp Arsenal in the 19th year (1893) of Guangxu of the Qing Dynasty. Today, it is still well-preserved. Its effective range is up to 16,000 meters (the longest range is 19,670 meters). It once was identified as "the world's oldest and largest coastal cannon in the 19th century on the original site".

英雄三岛

　　英雄三岛即大嶝岛观光游览区，位于翔安区大嶝街道，由大嶝岛、小嶝岛、角屿三个岛屿组成，点缀在灵动的浯江中，是厦（门）金（门）海域一颗瑰丽的明珠。在20世纪70年代以前，这里是军事禁区。观光园内有"世界最大军事广播喇叭""八二三炮阵地遗址""战地坑道"等景点。

　　"不到长城非好汉，不到三岛非英雄"。近年来，英雄三岛渐渐揭开神秘的面纱，昔日戒备森严的军事禁区成了宾客如云的旅游观光点，是全国唯一的集战地观光、爱国教育、休闲娱乐等为一体的教育基地和旅游胜地。

Three Hero Islands

　　The Three Hero Islands, also known as the Dadeng Sightseeing Area, are located at Dadeng Sub-district in Xiang'an district. It is composed of Dadeng Island, Xiaodeng Island and Jiaoyu Island. Embellished in the beautiful Wujiang River, it is a magnificent pearl in Xia(men) and Jin(men) sea area. Before the 1970s, this place was a restricted military area. There are many scenic spots in the park, such as "the world's largest horn", "the ruined places after Kinmen Bomb", and "the battlefield tunnel".

　　"If you don't go to the Great Wall, you are not a good man. If you don't go to Three Islands, you are not a hero." In recent years, the Three Hero Islands began to reveal their mysterious mask. The military restricted area that used to be strictly guarded now become a scenic spot for thousands of tourists. It is the only educational base and tourist destination that has all functions such as sightseeing, patriotic education and entertainment in the whole country.

4 信俗 Local Customs

南普陀寺

千年古刹南普陀寺坐落在厦门岛东南隅五老峰麓，始建于唐代末期，当时称泗洲寺；明代扩建殿堂，规模粗具；清初重修，因其面临碧澄海港，供奉观世音菩萨，与浙江普陀山观音道场类似，又在普陀山以南，得名"南普陀寺"，为闽南佛教圣地。闽南古语"一年走南普，三年免受苦，一餐平安菜，吉祥如意在"，此处的"南普"即为南普陀寺。

南普院寺坐北朝南，依山面海而建，规模宏大，气势庄严，中轴线主建筑为天王殿、大雄宝殿、乐途殿、大悲殿、藏经阁。其中，天王殿位于寺院中轴线的最前端，前殿正中供奉笑容可掬的弥勒佛，两侧立有怒目环视的四大天王，殿后有韦陀菩萨覆掌按杵而立，威武异常。

南普陀寺不仅是全国重点寺院，也是厦门著名风景区。这里一年四季郁郁葱葱，美丽如画。

Nanputuo Temple

Nanputuo Temple, with thousands of years of history, is located at the foot of the Wulao Peaks in the southeast end of Xiamen Island. It was built at the end of the Tang Dynasty and named Sizhou Temple at that time. In the Ming Dynasty, it extended its halls and began to take shape. In the Qing Dynasty, it was rebuilt. Since it faces the blue and clean harbor and enshrines Arya Avalokiteshvara, which is similar to the Avalokiteshvara Bodhimanda of Putuo Mountain in Zhejiang, and it is situated in the south of Putuo Mountain, it is named as "Nanputuo (South Putuo) Temple" and regarded as the Buddhist holy land of Fujian. In archaism of South Fujian, it said that "to stay at Nanpu for one year can keep you safe for three years and to eat a meal with safe meaning here can bring good fortunes as one wishes." Here, the "Nanpu" refers to "Nanputuo".

Facing south, Nanputuo Temple was built around the sea and mountains. With grand scale, it presents solemnity. The main buildings at the axle wire are Hall of Heavenly Kings, the Great Buddha's Hall, Letu Hall, the Great Compassion Hall and Depositarry of Buddhist Texts, among which, Hall of Heavenly Kings is located at the very front of the axle wire of the temple. In the front hall, Maitreya Buddha with broad smiles are enshrined and Four Heavenly Kings with glaring eyes stand on two sides. At the back of the hall, Wei Tuo Bodhisattva clasps hands and stands with pestles, which seems mighty and powerful.

Nanputuo Temple is not only a national key monastery, but also a famous scenic spot in Xiamen. It has been luxuriantly green all the year round like a beautiful picture.

梵天寺

梵行庄严广植德本，天人归仰常转法轮。

大轮山，是同安区内的主要山峰，层峦起伏，横亘数里，状为车轮滚动，奔跃而来，故名。

大轮山南麓的梵天寺，创建于隋开皇元年（581年），原名兴教寺，是福建最早的佛教寺庙之一，厦门岛内的妙释寺、鼓浪屿日光岩寺均是其分禅。

梵天寺历尽沧桑，但历代高僧辈出，雅士云集，香火绵延，声名远扬。著名的弘一法师和台湾佛学泰斗印顺导师曾挂单梵天寺。寺内有一宋代婆罗门佛塔，是福建省第一批文物保护单位。

Brahma Temple

The solemnity of brahmacariya cultivates morality and happiness extensively, and the celestials spread Buddhism frequently.

Dalun Mountain is the main peak in Tong'an District. It rolls and lies across miles away like the rolling wheels, which is the origin of its name.

Brahma Temple is located at the southern foot of Dalun Mountain, which was established in the 1st year of Kaihuang of the Sui Dynasty (581). Its primitive name is Xingjiao Temple, which is one of the earliest Buddhist temples in Fujian. Both of Miaoshi Temple in Xiamen Island and Sunlight Rock Temple in Gulangyu Island are its branches.

Even though Brahma Temple has experienced many vicissitudes of life, it cultivated many eminent monks, attracted refined scholars, gathered unceasing burning incense and enjoyed a widespread reputation. The distinguished Master Hong Yi and the Master Yinshun who is the leading authority in the Buddhist studies in Taiwan have once stayed in Brahma Temple. In the temple, there is a Brahman pagoda of the Song Dynasty, which has been treated as the first batch of officially protected sites in Fujian Province.

保生大帝信俗

保生大帝祥光聚，天地赐恩民寿康。

保生大帝为闽南、潮汕地区所信奉，俗称"大道公""吴真人""花桥公"。他是福建沿海普受人们尊奉的医仙，庙宇林立于中国大陆、台湾地区以及东南亚国家。其中，青礁慈济宫和白礁慈济宫被公认为是保生大帝的祖庙。

保生大帝姓吴名夲，宋代同安县人。自幼学医，精通医术，一生悬壶济世，行医救人无数，受到人们的敬仰和爱戴。绍兴二十一年（1151年），乡人合力在他制药行医的青礁龙湫坑修建了"龙湫庵"，雕塑神像，祀奉"医灵真人"，香火日盛。乾道二年（1166年），朝廷赐庙额"慈济"，现为海沧青礁慈济宫，迄今已有八百多年历史。

Belief in Life Protection Emperor

Blessed by Life Protection Emperor, people live a healthy and long life.

Life Protection Emperor, commonly referred to as "Dadaogong", "Wuzhenren" or "Huajiaogong", is the god worshiped by people across South Fujian and the Chaozhou-Jieyang-Shantou region. He is believed to be an immortal who mastered medical science by people in Fujian coastal areas. Temples in his name have been built across the Chinese mainland, Taiwan and Southeast Asia. Among them, the Qingjiao Tzu Chi Temple and Baijiao Tzu Chi Temple are recognized as the ancestral shrines of Life Protection Emperor.

Life Protection Emperor, originally named Wu Tao, was born in Tong'an County in the Song Dynasty. He studied medicine since childhood and practiced medicine. He saved numerous people throughout his life. His proficient skill and benevolent heart won him enormous admiration and love. In the 21st year of Shaoxing of the Song Dynasty (1151), local people worked together to build the "Longqiu An" in the Qingjiao Longqiu Pit, where he practiced his pharmaceutical career. His statue called "Medicine Spirit Immortal" in the temple was set up to memorize his medical life. Incense was burnt and there was a growing number of worshipers. In the 2nd year of Qiandao of the Song Dynasty (1166), the royal court granted the temple the title "Tzu Chi". The temple, now called Haicang Qingjiao Tzu Chi Temple, has a history of more than 800 years.

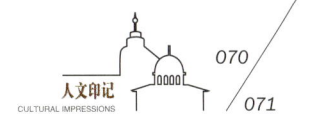

池王信俗

池王爷姓池，名然，南京人，为人耿直，居官清正，常怀治国安民、扶危济困之志。

相传明万历年间，他奉旨调任福建漳州府台，途经今翔安地界小盈岭，碰到两名使者。交谈后得知，这两人奉玉皇大帝之命，前往漳州播散瘟药，流布瘟疫，裁减人口。池然设计骗到瘟药吞服，以绝后患。走到马巷时，毒性发作，脸色变黑，在一棵大榕树下升天。玉皇大帝念池然宽厚仁慈，爱民如子，敕封"代天巡狩总制总巡王"，晋爵王爷，派往马巷为神。

明末清初郑成功收复台湾后，池王爷信仰传入宝岛及东南亚一带，至今已有三百多年历史，是台湾民间普遍信仰的神灵。

如今，翔安区马巷街上的元威殿，别名元威堂，俗称"池王宫"，主祀池王爷，为池王祖庙。

Belief in God Chi

God Chi, whose surname is Chi and given name is Ran, is from Nanjing. He is very upright in disciplining himself and fulfilling his official responsibilities. He always expected to run the country well and give the people peace and security.

According to the legend, he was transferred to be the magistrate of Zhangzhou, Fujian on imperial orders in the era of Wanli of the Ming Dynasty. He met two envoys when he passed Small Yingling Mountain, which is in present Xiang'an. After he communicated with them, he knew that they were going to disseminate drugs that could cause communicable diseases to Zhangzhou on the imperial order from the Jade Emperor (the Supreme Deity of Heaven) and to spread plague to cut down the population. Chi Ran tried to cheat them and swallowed the plague medicine himself to spare all troubles later on. When he arrived at Maxiang, he was toxic and his face turned black, then he died under a big banyan tree. Jade Emperor thought Chi Ran was generous and kind, who loved the people as his children, so Chi Ran was remitted and titled "the general imperial inspector representing the heaven", and was promoted as the royal highness and appointed as the God of Maxiang.

After Zheng Chenggong took back Taiwan between the end of the Ming Dynasty and the beginning of the Qing Dynasty, belief in God Chi has been transmitted to Taiwan and Southeast Asia. It has a history of over 300 years so far and God Chi has become the divinity worshiped by the public in Taiwan.

Nowadays, Yuanwei Temple at Maxiang Street in Xiang'an District has another name called Yuanwei Hall, which is commonly known as "Chi's Palace". This place is mainly used for worshiping God Chi, and it is the ancestral temple of God Chi.

福德文化

福德文化即土地公信仰。在民间，土地公也被视为财神与福神，因为民间相信"有土斯有财"，因此，土地公被当地人民奉为守护神。

仙岳山土地公庙历史悠久，始建于宋代，俗称"岩仔内土地公宫"，为塘边及周围百姓所建。明正德、万历、清同治、宣统年间，乡民屡次重修，筑石级山路抵庙，远近来拜，香火炽盛，逐渐形成祭祀民俗。

每年农历二月初二为土地公诞辰，闽南称"土地公生"。每月的农历初一、十五或初二、十六为月祭，每年的十二月十六为"尾牙"祭。民间活动有点头炷香仪式、请天公、颁典仪式、送炉、进香等，其中迎神踩街阵头和请戏谢神更是文化盛事。

Belief in Fude

Belief in Fude is the belief in God of Earth. In the folk lore of China, God of Earth is also regarded as God of Wealth and Blessing, because people believe that "land can bring wealth". Therefore, God of Earth is worshiped by the local people as patron their saint.

The temple of the God of Earth on Xianyue Mountain has a long history, which was established in the Song Dynasty. It is commonly known as "Palace of the God of Earth in Yanzainei". It was built by the common people living around Tangbian. During the era of Zhengde and Wanli of the Ming Dynasty and the era of Tongzhi and Xuantong of the Qing Dynasty, villagers rebuilt it several times and established the stone road to the temple. Many people came here to worship the god and burned incenses, which gradually formed the custom of sacrifice.

Every year, the second day of February of the lunar calendar is the birthday of the God of Earth. In Fujian, it is called "Birthday of God of Earth". The first day and the fifteenth day, or the second day and the sixteenth day of every month of the lunar calendar are the monthly sacrifice day. December 26 in every year is the sacrifice day of the "year–end dinner". Civil activities include the ceremony to light the first incense to invite the ruler of heaven, holding the sacrifice ceremony, sending stoves and offering incenses to Buddha and so on. Among these activities, meeting the deities, dancing performances, opera performed to show gratitude for gods are all cultural events.

5 人杰 Celebrities

苏颂

　　苏颂（1020—1101），福建同安县（今属厦门市同安区）人。北宋中期宰相，杰出的天文学家、天文机械制造家、药物学家。

　　苏颂好学，经史九流、百家之说，乃至于算法、地志、山经、本草、训诂、律吕等学，无所不通，医药学和天文学方面贡献突出。他领导制造世界上最古老的天文钟"水运仪象台"，开启近代钟表擒纵器的先河。李约瑟称其为"中国古代和中世纪最伟大的博物学家和科学家之一"。著有《图经本草》《新仪象法要》《苏魏公文集》等。苏颂在中国乃至世界都颇具知名度，是厦门在科学成就上的一张傲人名片。

Su Song

Su Song (1020-1101) came from Tong'an County (currently the Tong'an District), Fujian. He was the prime minister in the middle of the Song Dynasty, and also an eminent astronomer, astronomical instrument fabricator and pharmacologist.

Su Song was very studious, and he mastered history, classics, nine schools, doctrines of the ancient philosophers and even algorithm, chorography, mountain records, herbal medicine, exegesis, law and other studies. He also made a prominent contribution to medicine and astronomy. Under his leadership, China invented the world's oldest astronomical clock "astronomical clock tower", which pioneered the modern clockwork. Joseph Needham called him "one of the greatest naturalists and scientists in ancient China and the Middle Ages". He wrote many books, such as *Illustrations on Herbal Medicine*, *Law of New Clockwork*, *Collected Works of Su Song* and so on. Su Song is well-known in China and the world, who can represent the out-standing scientific achievement in Xiamen.

朱熹

朱熹（1130—1200），出生于南剑州尤溪（今属福建省尤溪县）。宋朝著名的理学家、思想家、哲学家、教育家、诗人，曾任同安县主簿，是闽学派的代表人物，儒学集大成者，世人尊称为朱子。

朱熹一生学而不厌，诲人不倦，博览经史，治学严谨，著作宏富。他在训诂、考证、注释古籍、整理文献资料等方面都取得了丰富的成果。在朱熹七年的仕途生涯中，厦门同安不仅是他的首仕之地，也是他任期最长的地方；他在同安期间完成了"逃禅归儒"的思想裂变，因而同安被看作是"朱子学"或"闽学"的发祥地。

Zhu Xi

Zhu Xi (1130–1200) was born in Youxi of Nanjianzhou (Youxi County of Fujian Province). He was a famous scholar, thinker, philosopher, educator and poet in the Song Dynasty. He once engaged as deputy governor of Tong'an County, who was the representative of Fujian school and also a Confucianism master. He was known as Zhu Zi by the world.

Zhu Xi was insatiable in learning and tireless in teaching in his life. He read classics and history extensively with a rigorous learning attitude, and wrote many books. He made rich achievements in exegesis, research, annotation of ancient books, collating literature and so on. In Zhu Xi's seven-year political career, Xiamen Tong'an was not only the first place for him to be an official, but also the place where he served for his longest term of office; during his stay in Tong'an, he completed his ideological fission of "converting from a Buddhist to a Confucian". Therefore, Tong'an is seen as the birthplace of "Zhu Zi School (Neo-Confucianism)" or "Min School".

郑成功

郑成功（1624—1662），福建泉州南安人，明末清初军事家、民族英雄。蒙隆武帝赐明朝国姓朱，赐名成功，永历帝封延平王。

清顺治二年（1645年）清军攻入江南，郑成功在东南沿海抗清，一度突袭、包围清江宁府（南京），遭击退后凭借海战优势固守海岛厦门、金门。清顺治十八年（1661年），郑成功率军横渡台湾海峡，翌年击败荷兰东印度公司在大员（今台湾台南市境内）的驻军，从荷兰侵略者手里收复沦陷38年的中国领土台湾。

为了纪念郑成功的历史功绩，福建省政府和厦门市政府在鼓浪屿建造郑成功纪念园，郑成功巨型石像于1985年落成。

Zheng Chenggong

Zheng Chenggong (1624-1662) was from Nan'an, Quanzhou of Fujian, who was a military strategist at the late Ming and early Qing Dynasties and a national hero. Emperor Longwu gave him the imperial family surname "Zhu" of the Ming Dynasty and the first name "chenggong", and Emperor Yongli awarded him the Yanping King.

In the 2nd year of Shunzhi of the Qing Dynasty (1645), Qing's army conquered the regions south of Yangtze River. Zheng Chenggong fought against Qing's army in China's southeastern coastal area. He once struck and sieged Jiangning of the Qing Dynasty (Nanjing of the former Ming Dynasty). After being repulsed, he defended the islands of Xiamen and Jinmen firmly by virtue of the naval advantage. In the 18th year of Shunzhi of the Qing Dynasty (1661), Zheng Chenggong led his troops to cross the Taiwan Strait and defeated the garrison from Dutch East India Company in Dayuan (now Taiwan Tainan City) and took back China's territory of Taiwan which had been occupied for 38 years by the Dutch invaders.

In order to commemorate Zheng Chenggong's historical achievements, the Fujian provincial government and the Xiamen municipal government constructed Zheng Chenggong Memorial Park in Gulangyu Island, in which Zheng Chenggong's giant stone statue was completed in 1985.

陈化成

陈化成（1776—1842），福建同安县（今属厦门市同安区）人，为同安丙洲陈氏的十五世子孙。出身行伍，历任参将、总兵。据史料记载，陈化成为官期间体恤百姓、关心民生，经常帮助穷困的百姓和士兵，自己却过着简朴的生活，并用积攒下来的钱为家乡出版了一部《厦门志》。鸦片战争爆发时陈化成任福建水师提督，驻守厦门；后改任江南提督保卫吴淞（今属上海市宝山区），与英国侵略军力战，英勇牺牲殉国。

Chen Huacheng

Chen Huacheng (1776-1842) was from Tong'an County of Fujian (now Xiamen Tong'an District), who was the child of the fifteenth generation of Chen's family at Bingzhou, Tong'an. He was once a soldier, who has served as senior soldier and commander-in-chief. According to historical records, Chen Huacheng showed solicitude for people, was concerned about the people's livelihood, and often helped the poor people and soldiers during his tenure, but he lived a simple life. He saved his money to publicize a book called *The Annals of Xiamen* for his hometown. Chen Huacheng was Fujian's navy commander-in-chief during the Opium War and stationed in Xiamen; Later, he was appointed as the commander-in-chief of the regions to the southern of Yangtze River, protecting Wusong (now Baoshan District of Shanghai) and fought with British invading army. At last, he died as a hero to defend the country.

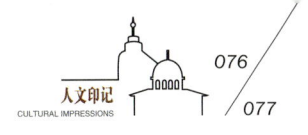

卢戆章

卢戆章（1854—1928），福建同安人，清末学者，创制中国切音新字，中国近现代著名新文字改革先驱，毕生从事语言文字研究和改革活动。

曾参加翻译《华英字典》。率先提出汉字拼音方案，并在推广"京音官话"（普通话）、推行汉字横排横写、提倡新式标点和简体字等方面开了先河。清光绪十八年（1892年），出版《一目了然新阶》，是中国人编著的第一本拼音著作。

1928年，卢戆章逝世，葬于鼓浪屿，其墓园被列为国家文物保护单位。

Lu Zhuangzhang

Lu Zhuangzhang (1854–1928) was from Tong'an of Fujian. He was the scholar at the end of the Qing Dynasty, who created phonetic Chinese alphabets. He was the famous pioneer of the New Writing Reform in the recent and modern China, who spent a lifetime on language research and reform.

He participated in the translation of the *Chinese and English Dictionary*. He set the precedent of the Chinese phonetic alphabet and acted as a pioneer in promoting "Beijing pronunciation and Mandarin language" (Mandarin), crosswise horizontal writings, new punctuation and simplified Chinese characters and so forth. In the eighteenth year of Guangxu of the Qing Dynasty (1892), he published *A Clarified New Phase*, which was the first book on Pinyin compiled by Chinese.

In 1928, Lu Zhuangzhang passed away and was buried in Gulangyu Island. His cemetery has been listed as a national officially protected site.

郁约翰

郁约翰（1861—1910），生于荷兰，长于美国。清光绪十四年（1888年）以医疗传教士身份来华。他是近代闽南第一所西医医院救世医院和妇女医院威赫敏娜医院的创办者；是第一所近代西医医学专科学校和护士专科学校的奠基者。他培养了黄大辟、陈天恩、陈伍爵、林安邦等厦门第一批西医人才。

郁约翰还是优秀的建筑师，漳州小溪医院及鼓浪屿救世医院均由他设计并建造，他还协助设计了鼓浪屿著名建筑——"八卦楼"和"船屋"。

1910年春，厦门鼠疫流行，郁约翰冒着生命危险救治病人，不幸感染。数日后去世，安葬于鼓浪屿"番仔公墓"。

Dr. John Abraham Otte

Dr. John Abraham Otte (1861–1910) was born in the Netherlands and grew up in the United States. In the fourteenth year of Guangxu of the Qing Dynasty (1888) he went to China as a medical missionary. He was the founder of Hope Hospital, the first Western medicine hospital in South Fujian, and the founder of the women's hospital Wilhelmina Hospital in recent era. Moreover, he was the founder of the first modern Western medicine college and nurses' college in recent era. He trained the first batch of Western medicine talents in Xiamen, such as Huang Dapi, Chen Tian'en, Chen Wujue and Lin Anbang.

Dr. John Abraham Otte was also an excellent architect, who designed and built the Zhangzhou Creek Hospital and Gulangyu Hope Hospital. He also helped to design two famous buildings in Gulangyu Island, namely the "Eight Diagrams Tower" and the "Boat House".

In the spring of 1910, a plague outbroke in Xiamen. Dr. John Abraham Otte tried to save patients by risking his own life. However, he was unfortunately infected, and died a few days later. He was buried in Gulangyu's "Foreigners' Cemetery".

黄仲涵

　　黄仲涵（1866—1924），祖籍福建同安，著名印尼华侨企业家。

　　20世纪初，黄仲涵继承父亲产业，成为响当当的"印尼糖王"。靠"一体化发展"的经营要诀，黄仲涵的"糖业帝国"不但顶住了实力强大的荷兰、日本等同行的竞争压力，而且迅速发展壮大，占印尼国内消费市场的一半左右，在国际市场上也占有一定份额，其公司在甘蔗种植、航运、金融业等产业的业务也具有相当规模。他的私人资产估计为千亿荷盾以上，他是继张弼士之后而早于陈嘉庚的又一华商顶尖巨富，是20世纪初影响最大的华商。

Huang Zhonghan

Huang Zhonghan (1866–1924), whose ancestral home was Tong'an of Fujian, is a famous Indonesian overseas Chinese entrepreneur.

At the beginning of the 20th century, Huang Zhonghan inherited his father's property and became the well-known "Indonesian Sugar King". With the "integrated development" operating tips, Huang Zhonghan's "Sugar Empire" not only withstood the competition pressure from peers in Netherlands, Japan and other countries, but also developed rapidly. His sugar mills accounted for about half of the domestic consumer market in Indonesia and also occupied a certain share in the international market. The expanded business to sugar cane cultivation, shipping and financial industry also reached a considerable scale. His private assets were estimated to be more than 100 billion Dutch guilders, which made him another top Chinese millionaire after Zhang Bishi and before Chen Jiageng. He was the most influential Chinese businessman in the 20th century.

陈嘉庚

陈嘉庚（1874—1961），著名的爱国华侨领袖、企业家、教育家、慈善家、社会活动家，同安县集美社人。

1913年回家乡集美先后创办集美小学、集美中学、师范、水产、航海、商科、农林等校（统称集美学校）和厦门大学。厦门大学、集美学校各校师生都尊称其为"校主"。

陈嘉庚一生爱国兴学，投身救亡斗争，推动华侨团结，争取民族解放，是侨界一代领袖和楷模。曾被毛泽东誉为"华侨旗帜、民族光辉"。

陈嘉庚毕生的实践形成内涵丰富的"嘉庚精神"，包括重义轻利、公而忘私的奉献精神；诚实守信、嫉恶好善的重德精神；刚健果毅、坚忍不拔的自强精神；艰苦朴素、勤勉节俭的清廉精神；与时俱进、革故鼎新的创新精神。

Chen Jiageng

Chen Jiageng (1874-1961), the famous patriotic overseas Chinese leader, entrepreneur, educator, philanthropist and social activist also known as Tan Kah Kee, was from Jimei, Tong'an County.

In 1913, he returned his hometown Jimei and founded Jimei Primary School, Jimei Secondary School, Jimei Normal School and other schools of aquatic products, navigation, business, agriculture and forestry (collectively Jimei School) and Xiamen University. Teachers and students from Xiamen University and Jimei School all respectfully address him as the "school master".

In his entire life, Cheng Jiageng loved the country and focused on promoting education. He actively devoted himself to saving the nation from being colonized, promoted the cooperation of overseas Chinese and fought for the national liberation. He was the leader and model of a generation of overseas Chinese, who was once honored as the "flag of overseas Chinese and pride of the nation" by Mao Zedong.

Chen Jiageng's life-wide practice forms the rich connotation of "Jiageng Spirit", including the spirit of utter devotion to justice above material gains and selflessness in the interest of the public; moral-oriented spirit to be honest and trustworthy and to praise the good and discard the evil; self-improvement spirit to be energetic and perseverant; upright spirit to be hardworking, plainly-living, assiduous and frugal; innovative spirit to advance with times and make general reforms.

林尔嘉

林尔嘉（1875—1951），字菽庄，晚年号百忍老人。诗人、教育家、实业家，著名的鼓浪屿"菽庄花园"的主人，曾任厦门市政会会长。他是厦门抗英名将陈胜元五子陈宗美的嫡长子，6岁时过继给台湾板桥林家。

林尔嘉自幼聪敏好学，是民国年间在闽台两地负有声望的人物，对厦门的城市建设多有建树，并在实业救国、教育救国和抗日中做出突出贡献。作为诗人，他发起成立菽庄吟社，编辑出版《菽庄丛刻》等。

林尔嘉对故乡的教育事业也极为关心，由他创办或在他支持下兴办的有厦门师范学堂、漳州师范学校、华侨女子学校。林尔嘉还是香港大学的捐创人之一。

Lin Erjia

Lin Erjia (1875–1951), whose courtesy name was Shuzhuang and who was also known as Bairen Laoren in his later years, was a poet, educator and businessman. He was the owner of the famous "Shuzhuang Garden" in Gulangyu Island, and he was also the president of Xiamen municipal administration council. He was the first son of Chen Zongmei and his first wife, and his father was the fifth son of the celebrated anti-British general Chen Shengyuan. When Lin Erjia was six years old, he was adopted by the Lin family at Banqiao in Taiwan.

Lin Erjia had been smart and studious in his childhood. Later, he became a prestigious character in Fujian and Taiwan during the period of the Republic of China. He realized great achievements in Xiamen's urban construction. He had also made great contributions to saving the nation by engaging in industry and education as well as the anti-Japan wars. As a poet, he initiated the establishment of Shuzhuang Poetry Society, and edited and published the *Collected Works of Shuzhuang*.

Lin Erjia was also very concerned about the education in his hometown, and founded or supported the establishment of Xiamen Normal School, Zhangzhou Normal School, Overseas Chinese Women School. Lin Erjia was also one of the donors of Hong Kong University.

马约翰

马约翰（1882—1966），生于鼓浪屿。著名现代体育教育家，清华大学体育教授。

1905年，他曾代表中国获"上海万国田径运动会"一英里赛冠军。1936年，出任中国体育代表团总教练，带领中国队参加在柏林举行的第十一届夏季奥林匹克运动会。1954年起任中国田径协会主席，中华全国体育总会副主席、主席。

马约翰终生坚持体育锻炼，身体非常健康，年逾八十，鹤发童颜，仍生气勃勃地工作，被誉为"提倡体育运动的活榜样"。他一生积极倡导体育，热情指导青年进行体育锻炼，发表过《体育运动的迁移价值》《我们对体育应有的认识》等论著，被称为"我国体育界的一面旗帜"。

Ma Yuehan

Ma Yuehan (1882-1966) was born in Gulangyu Island. He was a famous modern sports educator and sports professor in Tsinghua University.

In 1905, he won the championship in the one-mile race of "Shanghai Universal Athletics Games" on behalf of China. In 1936, as the head coach of Chinese sports delegation, he led Chinese players to attend the 11th Olympic Games held in Berlin. Since 1954, He had served as the chairman of the Chinese Athletic Association, and the vice chairman and chairman of the All China Sports Federation.

Ma Yuehan insisted on physical exercise in his whole life and was always in good health. When he was over eighty years old, he looked very young and still worked vigorously, known as "the living example of promoting sports". He actively advocated sports in his life and enthusiastically guided young people to do physical exercise and published several works such as *Migration Value of Sports* and *Our Understandings of Sports*, known as "the banner in China's sports world".

林巧稚

林巧稚（1901—1983），生于鼓浪屿，医学家。她在胎儿宫内呼吸、女性盆腔疾病、妇科肿瘤、新生儿溶血症等方面的研究做出了贡献，是中国妇产科学的主要开拓者、奠基人。

林巧稚是北京协和医院第一位中国籍妇产科主任及首届中国科学院唯一的女学部委员（院士），虽然一生未婚，却亲自接生5万多婴儿，被尊称为"万婴之母""生命天使""中国医学圣母"。2009年9月14日，林巧稚被评为100位中华人民共和国成立以来感动中国人物之一。

林巧稚逝世后，厦门鼓浪屿于1984年5月建造了名为"毓园"的林巧稚纪念馆。

Lin Qiaozhi

Lin Qiaozhi (1901-1983) was born in Gulangyu Island and was a medical scientist. She has made contribution to the studies on fetal breathing in intrauterine, female pelvic disease, gynecologicaloncology and hemolytic disease of the newborn and other diseases. She was the main pioneer and founder of China's obstetrics and gynecology.

She was the first native director of Department of Obstetrics and Gynecology in Peking Union Medical College Hospital, and the only female academician of the first session of the Chinese Academy of Sciences (CAS). Although she was never married, she delivered over 50,000 babies in her career, known as "Mother of Ten Thousands of Babies", "Life Angel" and "Holy Mother of Chinese Medicine". On September 14, 2009, she was named as one of the one hundred people of Touching China since the founding of the People's Republic of China.

After her death, Gulangyu Island of Xiamen built the Lin Qiaozhi Memorial Hall named "Yuyuan Garden" in May 1984.

卢嘉锡

卢嘉锡（1915—2001），福建厦门人，著名科学家、教育家和社会活动家，中国科学院院长，是中国结构化学学科的开拓者与奠基人。

1928年，13岁的卢嘉锡考入厦门大学预科组；19岁，卢嘉锡完成了化学和数学双主系的学习，成为"双学士"；21岁后，卢嘉锡又先后赴伦敦大学、加州理工学院深造。1944年，卢嘉锡到美国国防委员会从事战时军事科学研究。1945年，怀抱"科学救国"远大抱负的卢嘉锡回到母校厦大任化学系主任，在他四处争取资金、搜集药品设备、网罗师资人才的努力下，厦大化学系很快崛起。1981年至1987年，卢嘉锡任中国科学院院长，并当选为第三世界科学院副院长。

卢嘉锡一生崇尚科学，勇于创新，以"科教兴国"为己任，"固氮（即科研）"不辍，"育人"不已，是科学巨擘，亦是师表楷模。

Lu Jiaxi

Lu Jiaxi (1915-2001), born in Xiamen, Fujian, well-known scientist, educator and social activist, former president of the Chinese Academy of Sciences, and the pioneer and founder of China's structural chemistry.

In 1928, Lu Jiaxi, 13 years old, passed the entrance examination to a preparatory class of Xiamen University. When he was 19 years old, he completed the study of two majors, chemistry and mathematics, and got Double Bachelor's Degrees. After he was 21 years old, he further studied in the University of London and California Institute of Technology. In 1944, he was engaged in wartime military science research in the US National Defense Research Committee (NDRC). In 1945, embracing the ambition of "saving China by science", he returned to China and was appointed as the dean of the Chemistry Department at Xiamen University. This department rose rapidly after his attracting funds, collecting medicines and equipment and recruiting teachers. He served as the president of the Chinese Academy of Sciences (CAS) from 1981 to 1987, and also as vice president of the Third World Academy of Sciences.

He advocated science and strived to make innovations in his life, treated "invigorating China through science and education" as responsibility, and relentlessly continued to do scientific research and education work. He is a scientific giant and a model for teachers.

陈景润

陈景润（1933—1996），世界著名数学家，被称为"科学怪人"。1953 年，陈景润毕业于厦门大学，1954 年调回厦门大学任资料员，同时研究数论，1956 年调入中国科学院数学研究所，1980 年当选中科院物理学数学部委员。

他凭羸弱之躯，在异常艰难的条件下，忍受常人难以想象的病痛和折磨，耗尽毕生心血去追求一个几近不可能的梦想——攻克"哥德巴赫猜想"中的"1+2"。他的研究结果受到世界数学界的高度重视和称赞，英国数学家哈博斯坦姆和德国数学家李希特把陈景润的成果写进数学书中，称为"陈氏定理"。他所取得的成就使他成为当时全社会的传奇人物，影响了当时中国整整一代人，并因此获得了英雄般的赞誉和荣耀。

Chen Jingrun

Chen Jingrun (1933-1996) was a world famous mathematician and known as the "scientific oddity". In 1953, he graduated from Xiamen University. In 1954, he was appointed as a documenter and studied number theory in Xiamen University. In 1956, he worked in the Institute of Mathematics of the Chinese Academy of Sciences, and was elected to be the member of the Department of Mathematical Physics of the Chinese Academy of Sciences in 1980.

With his frail body and under extremely difficult conditions, he endured the pain and suffering which was unimaginable for ordinary people and exhausted his lifelong efforts to pursue a nearly impossible dream, namely, to verify the "1 plus 2" in "Goldbach Conjecture". His research results were highly valued and praised by the world's mathematical community. The British mathematician Halberstam (H. Halberstam) and German mathematician Richert (H. E. Richert) included his findings into their mathematics book, which were called "Chen's Theorem". His achievements made him the legend of the whole society at that time, influenced the whole generation of China lived in that period and gained him heroic praise and glory.

许斐平

　　许斐平（1952—2001），生于鼓浪屿，中央乐团旅美钢琴家，被认为是中国钢琴界少数的几个天才之一。20世纪70年代末，成为中央音乐学院的首席钢琴独奏。1979年，获得奖学金进入美国伊斯曼音乐学院，次年转入著名的茱莉亚学院。1983年，获钢琴界最悠久的赛事——鲁宾斯坦国际钢琴赛金奖，这也是继刘诗昆之后，20年来首位获此殊荣的华人钢琴家。1989年，许斐平进入华盛顿肯尼迪中心演出，意味着他进入世界一流钢琴家行列。《纽约时报》和《华盛顿邮报》称他为"钢琴界的国际之星"。

Fei-Ping Hsu (Xu Feiping)

　　Fei-Ping Hsu (1952-2001), born in Gulangyu Island, was a pianist of Central Orchestra who lived in America for a long time, and was considered as one of the few geniuses in Chinese piano sector. In the late 1970s, he became the chief piano soloist of the Central Conservatory of Music. In 1979, he got the scholarship to study in the American Eastman School of Music and then attended the famous Juilliard School in 1980. In 1983, he was a Gold Medal winner at the Arthur Rubinstein International Piano Competition which was the competition in piano sector with the longest history, the first Chinese pianist won the competition in 20-year history after Liu Shikun getting this award. In 1989, he performed in the John F. Kennedy Arts Center in Washington, which meant that he was one of the world first-class pianists. The *New York Times* and the *Washington Post* called him the "International Star of Piano".

FOUR

风物匠心
INCREDIBLE CUSTOMS AND INGENIOUS CRAFTSMANSHIP

厦门,这里承载**风物匠心**、声影手作在味蕾中绽放传承不变初心。

Boasting incredible customs and ingenious craftsmanship, Xiamen has bloomed together with its unchanged traditions.

4

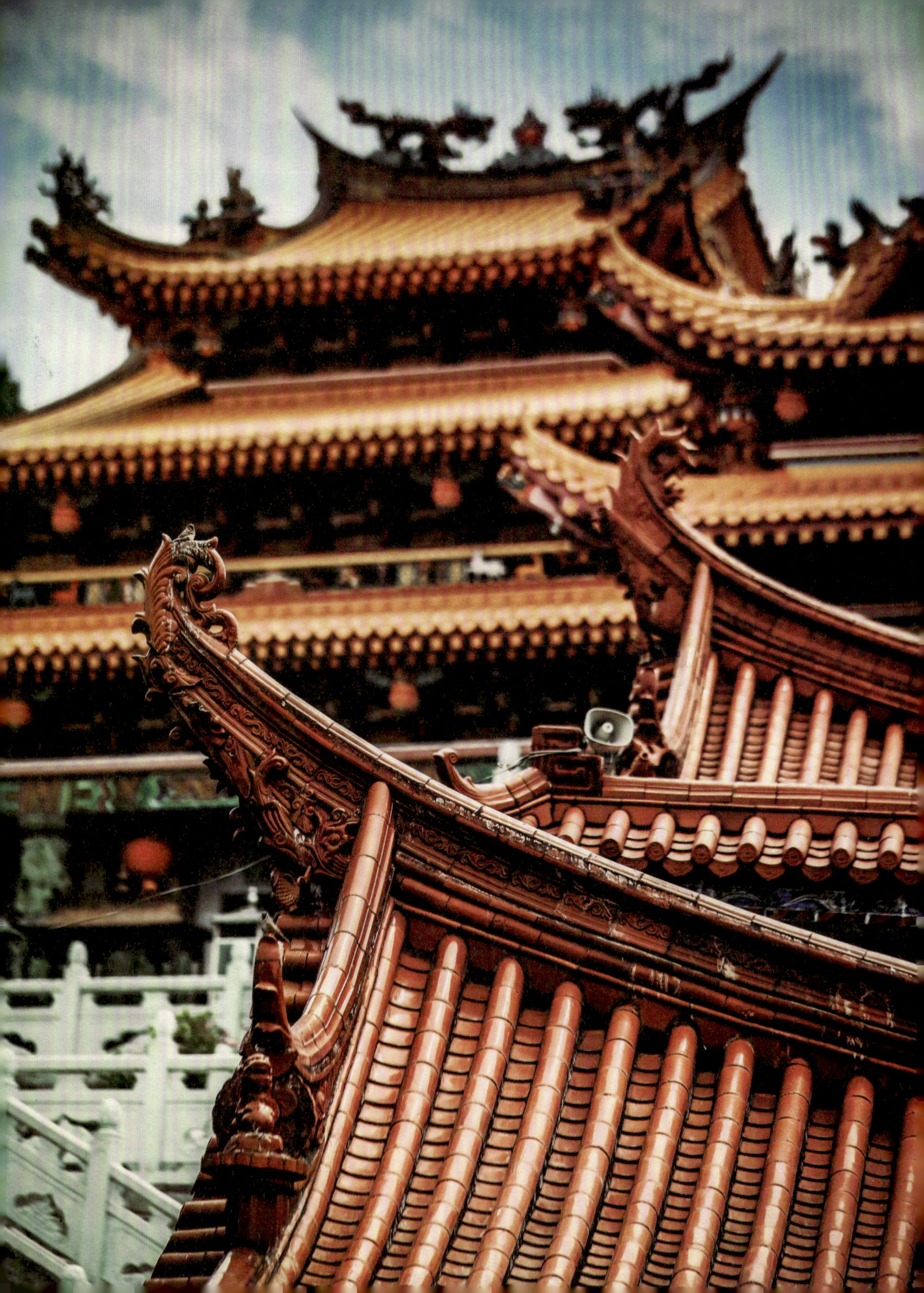

城市如人，既是物质的，也是精神的。有过去，有现在，也有未来；有共性，有个性，更有追求。

刘易斯·芒福德在《城市文化》中说：城市是文化的容器。

时光的脚步在闽南这古老而又神奇的土地上来了又回，看着它们穿过漏窗，把风影镂刻于红砖的墙壁，而后在大海的余晖中追逐着远去。

有着对经典的传承，更有令人惊艳的创新：最富地方特色的民谣；著名的漆线雕、珠绣等民间工艺美术；被誉为"宋元南戏活化石"的南音；中国八大方言之一的闽南语……无一不向我们昭示着闽南地方厚博的历史积淀与人文智慧。

跟着舌尖来旅行，厦门是一个美食天堂，厦门菜肴创出清、鲜、淡、脆略带微辣的独特风味，尤以生猛海鲜、仿古药膳、普陀素菜、风味小吃著称。坐在街边巷尾不起眼的小店里，吃上一碗热腾腾的沙茶面，品的是各种好料，呷的是浓香的汤头，享受的是内心的那份温暖、闲适与安宁。刚上岸的本港小海鲜，买完后直接加工，简单做个酱油水，然后在海边支张小桌子，悠闲而自在，不挤又不闹，这才是在厦门生活的样子。

这些成熟的、世俗的、欢乐的、亮彩的活力因子，丰富着、塑造着城市。在不同文化碰撞中，在不断的时代融合中，我们听见厦门拔节生长的声音。

City is both material and spiritual, just like human. It has past, present and future, and has commonalities, personality and aspiration.

Lewis Mumford said in *The Culture of Cities* that city was the container of culture.

The footsteps of time go back and forth on this ancient and magical land of South Fujian. They run through the leaking windows, carve the shadow of the wind in the red brick walls, and then chase away in the afterglow of the sea.

Various aspects of this city show us its historical accumulation and human wisdom of South Fujian, including both the heritage of the classics and amazing innovations, ballads with local characteristics, famous folk arts and crafts such as lacquer thread sculpture and bead embroidery, Nanyin Music which is called the "living fossil of the Southern Opera in the Song and Yuan dynasties", and the South Fujian language as one of China's eight major dialects.

Following your tongue to travel, Xiamen is a gourmet paradise. Xiamen cuisine tastes mild, fresh, light, crisp and a little spicy, and is distinguished for fresh seafood, antique medicinal cuisine, Putuo vegetables and snacks. Sitting in the small shops located in the trampled edges of streets, you can eat a bowl of Sate Noodles. What you taste is a variety of good ingredients. What you sip is the fragrant soup. What you enjoy is the warmth, leisure and tranquility of heart. The seafood which just lands from local port is processed directly after being bought, accompanied by the simple mixture of soy sauce and water. Then you can place a small table at the seaside to enjoy the cuisine. This kind of leisure and comfortable life is the real life in Xiamen, not crowded or noisy.

These mature, secular, cheerful and bright vitality factors enrich and shape the city. In the collision of different cultures and the constant integration of different times, we can hear the sound of the rapid development of Xiamen.

七桃

虾米碗糕

没法度

话仙

灰熊

1 传承 Inheritance

闽南方言

自汉魏开始，历经南北朝、唐宋等时期，北方汉人因各种原因不断迁徙到南方地区，其中一部分进入闽南地区。他们把北方各时期汉语的语音词语与闽地少数民族的语言文化进行融合，逐渐形成和发展成以汉语为主体的闽南地域方言，这就是闽南话。

闽南话是超地区、超省界的汉语方言。它主要通行于闽南地区、粤东的潮汕地区和台湾省的大部分地区。千余年来，闽南、潮汕一带有不少人出洋谋生而相继向外移居。人语相随，今天的东南亚诸国，有相当部分华侨和华裔仍然以闽南方言作为他们的交际工具。

闽南方言分布广泛，究其"正宗"，应是福建的泉州、漳州和厦门地区，而泉州方言则是早期闽南方言的代表。厦门话正好是泉漳之间的土语，正所谓"半漳半泉厦门腔"。

South Fujian Dialects

From the beginning of the Han and Wei Dynasties and through the Northern and Southern Dynasties, and the Tang and Song Dynasties, the northern Han people continued to migrate to the southern areas due to various reasons, and part of them moved to South Fujian. They merged Chinese phonetic words of the northern area in different dynasties with the language and culture of the minorities in Fujian, and gradually formed and developed the regional dialects of South Fujian with Chinese as the main body. This is South Fujian dialects.

South Fujian dialects are the trans-regional and trans-provincial Chinese dialects. They are mainly used in the South Fujian area, Chaoshan of eastern Guangdong and the most areas of Taiwan. For more than a thousand years, a large number of people in South Fujian and Chaoshan have moved outwards to make a living by going abroad. Language goes with people. In today's Southeast Asian countries, numerous overseas Chinese and foreign citizens with Chinese ancestry still use South Fujian dialects as their communication tools.

South Fujian dialects are widely distributed and the origin should be Quanzhou, Zhangzhou and Xiamen of Fujian Province. Quanzhou dialect is the representative of the early South Fujian dialects. Xiamen dialect is exactly the language between the Quanzhou dialect and the Zhangzhou dialect, which is the so-called "language of half Zhangzhou and half Quanzhou".

呷霸咩

米呆

冻未条

巴豆妖

瓦尬哩贡

歹势

工夫茶

厦门是工夫茶的起源地之一,拥有浓郁的茶文化氛围。厦门茶文化的精华是茶道,讲究五境之美,即茶叶、茶水、茶具、火候、环境。厦门人大多爱喝乌龙茶,尤以安溪铁观音为最爱,铁观音号称茶中极品,有诗盛赞:"珠泉隽味和胸臆,玉液新香沁齿牙,两腋清风瓯泛绿,一壶春雪笔生花。"

一泡高古绝俗、诗意盎然的工夫茶,只是厦门人每日开门七件事中的头一件稀松平常事。在厦门,无论你是朋友还是陌生人,无论你是走进高楼大厦还是洋房古厝,无论你是去办公室谈正经事还是在街市里闲逛,你足之所及、目之所至,嗅之所处,无不有这么一泡工夫茶,于君前后左右自在飘香。

厦门人泡茶,泡的是自己的心情,自己的品位,自己的气质;天天泡在此茶中的厦门人,自然泡出茶的神韵、茶的气度。

Kungfu Tea

Xiamen is one of the origins of kungfu tea with a strong cultural atmosphere of tea. The essence of Xiamen tea culture is tea ceremony, which involves five necessary elements: tea leaves, water, tea set, fire and environment. Xiamen people mostly drink Oolong tea and especially love Anxi Tieguanyin, which is known as the highest grade of tea and praised by a poem, "The flavor of tea lasts in chest after tasting; the fragrance of this jade liquid is left between teeth; the cup of tea looks green after blowing wind; and poets will write good after drinking this pot of spring snow".

Making the elegant and poetic kungfu tea is the first among the daily seven things done by Xiamen people after opening the door. In Xiamen, whether you are a friend or a stranger, whether you are walking into high buildings or ancient houses in western style, whether you are going to the office to talk about serious things or wandering in the streets of the city, there will be kungfu tea accessible for you to get, to see and to smell, which release fragrance around you.

Xiamen people make tea to relax their mood and improve their taste and temperament. Surrounded by tea in their everyday life, it is no wonder that Xiamen people have the charm and tolerance of tea.

讲古场

说书，闽南和厦门方言叫作"讲古"，说书艺人被称为"讲古仙"，说书的地方则被称为"讲古场"。

清道光《厦门志》说："讲古"——"说平话者，绿荫树下，古佛寺前，称说汉唐以来遗事，众人环听，敛钱为馈，可使愚顽不识字者为兴感之用……""讲古仙"手里只拿一本书，折扇或蒲扇。茶桌仔放着茶具，泡壶茶，讲渴时抿口茶。经验丰富的"讲古仙"则凭着口若悬河的生动语汇、丰富的面部表情和形象的动作，绘影绘色地"讲古"，引人入胜。

20世纪20年代，厦门"讲古"极盛时，开讲分早晚两场，座无虚席。1928年，岛上"讲古场"达50多处，遍布全市。

"讲古"在厦门是一项最典型、最平民化的传统文化，具有极强的生命力。随着时代的进步，社会文娱活动的现代化、多样化，"讲古场"的活动空间大大缩小。但是，它仍顽强地持续，并以新的传播形式适应、生存、发展着。

Jianggu Ground

Storytelling in South Fujian and Xiamen dialects is called "Jianggu", and storytellers are called "Jianggu Xian". The place of storytelling is called "Jianggu Ground".

In *The Annals of Xiamen* of the Daoguang reign in the Qing Dynasty, it is said that "people who speak Pinghua (a dialect used in the southwest China) tell the story after the Han and Tang dynasties under the trees and before the ancient Buddhist temples to make a living, surrounded by audiences, providing entertainment for people without education". "Jianggu Xian" only takes a book and a folding fan or palm-leaf fan in hand. There is tea set and a pot of tea on the table, so storyteller can drink when thirsty. Experienced "Jianggu Xian" tells stories vividly through his eloquent vocabulary, expressive facial expressions and gestures, which fascinates the audiences.

In 1920s, "Jianggu" developed to the climax in Xiamen. Stories would be told twice a day, morning and evening, and all seats would be occupied. In 1928, there were over 50 "Jianggu Grounds" on the island, scattered over the whole city.

"Jianggu" in Xiamen is the most typical and civilian traditional culture with a strong vitality. With the progress of the times, social recreational activities are modernized and diversified, resulting in the greatly reduced space for the development of "Jianggu Ground". But it is still tenacious to continue and adapts itself to survive and develop in the new form of dissemination.

中秋博饼

博饼，是厦门人几百年来独有的中秋传统活动，是独特的月饼文化，也是厦门人对历史的传承。

相传，中秋博饼，是郑成功屯兵时为解士兵的中秋相思之情、激励鼓舞士气，命部将洪旭发明的。于是，一代一代传下来，就成了如今厦门独具特色的民间习俗。每逢中秋佳节临近，灯火辉煌中的厦门，大街小巷便会传出博饼时骰子撞碰瓷碗的悦耳叮当声。

厦门博饼，讲究的就是一个开心，博个好兆头。博饼规则一般是5至10人一桌，以出现四颗红四点、两颗红一点为最高级，称"状元插金花"。大多数人都愿意相信，博中状元的人一年运气总是会特别好，这当然是因为博饼活动里倾注了人们的感情寄托。

Mid-Autumn Mooncake Gambling

Mooncake gambling is a traditional activity in the Mid-Autumn Festival held only by Xiamen people over the past hundreds of years, and a unique culture of mooncake, which is also the history legacy of Xiamen people.

It is said that Mid-Autumn mooncake gambling is invented by Hong Xu ordered by Zheng Chenggong who was intended to relieve the homesickness of soldiers in the Mid-Autumn Festival and boost their morale when stationed his troops. As a result, it is passed on from generation to generation and becomes a unique folk custom in Xiamen. Whenever the Mid-Autumn Festival is approaching, in the night of Xiamen, there will be melodious sound of dices hitting the bowl when mooncake gambling activities are held on streets.

Xiamen mooncake gambling is played to make happiness and wish for a good sign. The rule of this gambling is generally five to ten people at a table. And the situation of four red four-points and two red one-point is called "Zhuangyuan (champion) with gold flower". Most people are willing to believe that the people getting Zhuangyuan will be always in good luck in the next year, which is presumably because of the emotional sustenance people devote into the mooncake gambling activities.

赛龙舟

农历五月初五，厦门人称"五月节"，至今仍保留着吃粽子和赛龙舟的习俗。集美学校的龙舟池和市区筼筜湖是厦门组织龙舟竞赛的场所。竞赛时金鼓齐鸣，人声鼎沸，健儿们驾着颀长的七彩龙舟，劈波斩浪，奋勇争先，别有一番风情。

集美龙舟赛是陈嘉庚先生为纪念爱国诗人屈原亲自筹划和组织的。1951年端午节，第一届龙舟赛在海上举办，自1955年起改为在集美龙舟池举办。1985年海内外集美校友为缅怀集美学校校主陈嘉庚先生，继承和发扬其爱国主义精神，将集美龙舟赛冠名为"嘉庚杯"龙舟赛，并于1987年举办了首届"嘉庚杯"国际龙舟邀请赛。2006年起举办的"嘉庚杯""敬贤杯"海峡两岸龙舟赛，成为参赛规模较大、竞技水平较高的国家级龙舟赛事。

Dragon Boat Racing

The fifth day of the fifth lunar month is called "May Festival" by Xiamen people who still keep the custom of eating rice dumplings and holding dragon boat races at this festival. The dragon boat pool in Jimei School and Yundang Lake in the city are places to organize dragon boat races in Xiamen. When the races start, gongs and drums beat all around with the voices of numerous people, and paddlers drive the long colorful dragon boats to strive toward the forefront by paddling continuously, thus making it a unique landscape.

Jimei Dragon Boat Race was first planned and organized by Chen Jiageng personally to commemorate the patriotic poet Qu Yuan. At the Dragon Boat Festival of 1951, the first Dragon Boat Race was held on the sea, and the race has been shifted to the dragon boat pool of Jimei since 1955. In 1985, Jimei alumni at home and abroad changed the Jimei Dragon Boat Race into "Jiageng Cup" International Dragon Boat Race to honor the president of Jimei University, Chen Jiageng and inherit and develop his patriotic spirit, which was firstly held in 1987. "Jiageng Cup" and "Jingxian Cup" Cross-Strait Dragon Boat Race has been held since 2006, which is a national dragon boat tournament with a large scale and a high level.

送王船

大海苍茫，风助火势，火焰高腾，"王船"化吉近三小时，色彩鲜艳的纸偶、纸帆瞬间灰飞烟灭，船桅倒下，全船烧尽。金黄的火光照亮信徒们虔诚的面孔，他们面朝大海，手握线香，默默诵经。海水涨潮，将船灰卷进大海，漂向远方。

"送王船"又称"烧王船"，是沿海渔港、渔村的传统民俗，起于滨海渔村的"海醮"习俗，保留了较浓厚的原生态风味。

送王船送的是"代天巡狩"的王爷，王爷代替皇帝巡游四方，赏善罚恶，保佑风调雨顺、国泰民安。该习俗最早可追溯到明初，2011年被列入国家非物质文化遗产名录。

厦门"送王船"民俗活动，以湖里钟宅、同安吕厝、海沧钟山这三个地方的规模较大，三四年举行一次，固定农历月份中的某一天，寄托祛邪、避灾、祈福的美好愿望。

Sending off the Wang Boat

In the vast sea, the wind makes the fire get bigger and the flame higher. Praying with the "Wang Boat" for nearly three hours, colorful paper dolls and paper sails are instantly burnt into ashes, the masts fall down, and the whole ship is burnt out. The golden fire illuminates the devout faces of the believers, who face the sea, cling to the incenses, and chant silently. The rising tide of the sea engulfs the ashes into the sea and drifts to the distance.

"Sending off the Wang Boat" is also called "Burning the Wang Boat", which is the traditional folk custom of the fishing ports and fishing villages on coastal area. This originates from "Haijiao (maritime religious ceremonies)" custom in the coastal fishing villages and maintains a strong primitive flavor.

The ceremony aims to send off the royal highness of "imperial inspector representing the heaven", who cruised in the country for the emperor to reward the virtuous and punish the wicked, and to bless good weather for the crops and prosperous life for the people. This custom can be dated back to as early as the beginning of the Ming Dynasty. In 2011, it has been listed in the National Intangible Cultural Heritage.

This folk activity of "Sending off the Wang Boat" in Xiamen has a large scale in Zhongzhai of Huli, Lvcuo of Tong'an and Zhongshan of Haicang, which is held once in every three or four years at a fixed day in lunar calendar to carry the great expectations of eliminating evil, avoiding disasters and blessing.

2 手作 / Craftsmanship

漆线雕

　　厦门漆线雕是中国漆艺文化宝库中的艺术瑰宝之一，是闽南地区的汉族传统工艺。三百年前，同安县马巷镇就是漆线雕的制作基地。

　　自唐代彩塑兴盛以来，漆线雕便被应用于佛像装饰。漆线雕是以精细的漆线，经特殊的制作方法缠绕出各种金碧辉煌的人物及动物形象，尤以民间传统题材，如龙凤、麒麟、云水、缠枝莲等为多。漆线雕做工精细雅致，形象逼真生动，风格古朴庄重，画面栩栩如生，堪称艺苑奇葩，中国一绝。

　　2006年，漆线雕技艺被列入首批国家级非物质文化遗产名录。

Lacquer Thread Sculpture

　　The Lacquer Thread Sculpture of Xiamen is one of the art treasures in the Chinese treasure house of lacquer art. It is also a traditional handcraft of the Han people in the South Fujian areas. Three hundred years ago, Maxiang Town of Tong'an County is the production base of lacquer thread sculpture.

　　Since the Tang Dynasty when the painted sculpture flourished, lacquer thread sculpture has been used to decorate Buddha statues. The lacquer thread sculpture uses fine threads to twine around the glorious statues through special production methods. The traditional themes dominate the patterns, including dragon, phoenix, unicorn, cloud and lotus. The lacquer thread sculpture with its fine and delicate handcraft, vivid expressions and ancient style is regarded as one of the finest handcrafts only exists in the Chinese culture.

　　In 2006, the Lacquer Thread Sculpture was enlisted in the first National Intangible Cultural Heritage List.

珠绣

　　细小珍珠、玻璃珠、宝石珠等珠粒，纯手工绣在布上，具有珠光灿烂、绚丽多彩、层次清晰、立体感强的艺术特色，这就是珠绣。

　　厦门珠绣工艺的历史有近百年，早在20世纪20年代初期，华侨从海外带回玻璃珠点缀的绣花拖鞋，厦门民间制鞋艺人看了爱不释手，从中受到启发，设法从日本、南洋一带捎回一些玻璃珠子，开始尝试在鞋面上绣出各种花鸟图案。于是，厦门珠绣便开始流行开了。

　　厦门珠绣鼎盛期在20世纪七八十年代，各种产品出口到包括亚、欧、美50多个国家或地区，为厦门赢得了美誉。2007年，厦门珠绣被列入福建省级非物质文化遗产名录。

Bead Embroidery

　　The small pearls, glass beads, jewels and so on are embroidered on the cloth, which is purely handmade. With the shining glory, colorful decorations, clear layout and a strong sense of art with stereoscopic impression, it is named as "Bead Embroidery".

　　The bead embroidery in Xiamen has a hundred-year history. In the early 1920s, some overseas Chinese brought back slippers embroidered with glass beads from abroad. The craftsmen in Xiamen liked this decoration very much and were inspired by it. The craftsmen contrived to get some of these glass beads from Japan and Southeast Asia, and tried to embroider various kinds of bird and flower patterns on the shoes. Thus, the bead embroidery started to become a fashion style.

　　The fashion style reached its peak in the 1970s and 1980s. Many kinds of bead embroidery products were exported to more than fifty countries or regions in Asia, Europe and America, which won precious reputation for Xiamen. In 2007, the Xiamen Bead Embroidery was inlisted in the Fujian Provincial Intangible Cultural Heritage List.

3 声影 Opera

南音

　　许多人听过昆曲，甚至知道南戏，但对南音相对却陌生一些。

　　南音也称"弦管"，最早可以追溯到汉代，其后晋、唐、宋等朝代的中原汉族移民把音乐文化带入闽南地区，并与当地民间音乐融合。

　　"南音"乃就流传地域而言，"弦管"指南管音乐以丝竹箫弦为主要演奏乐器。南音始终保持着古代中原的古风古味，有"中国音乐史上的活化石"之称。那些大半都已湮灭无闻的唐音宋调，借助南音这个在民间口耳相传的"多媒体"孑遗，让现代人得以窥见一鳞半爪。随着闽南人向外迁徙，南音传到台湾、港澳和东南亚等地区和国家。在客居他乡的游子心中，南音就是华夏传统，就是精神故乡，是传唱不息的"乡音"。

　　2006年，南音经国务院批准列入第一批国家级非物质文化遗产名录；2009年南音正式被联合国教科文组织列入人类非物质文化遗产代表作名录。

Nanyin Music

Many people have heard the Kun opera and even knew the Southern Opera, but they are relatively unfamiliar with Nanyin music (the Southern music).

Nanyin is also called "Xianguan" (strings and woodwinds). It dates back earliest to the Han Dynasty, and then the Han migrants in the central plains of the Jin, Tang and Song Dynasties brought their own music to the southern Fuijan areas and integrated it with local folk music.

The name Nanyin refers to the geographical location where the music is popular, while Xianguan comes from the fact that the music of southern China are usually played with traditional stringed and woodwind instruments. Nanyin still keeps the ancient music style, which has the title of "the Living Fossil in the Chinese Music History". Most of the diminishing music of the Tang and Song Dynasties are heard by the modern people through the help of Nanyin. With the South Fujian people migrating to other places, Nanyin is spread to Taiwan, Hong Kong, Macao and Southeast Asian countries. In the hearts of the overseas Chinese, Nanyin is the tradition of Huaxia, the spirit hometown and the sounds of home.

In 2006, Nanyin was enlisted in the first National Intangible Cultural Heritage List under the approval of the State Council; in 2009, Nanyin was officially enlisted into the "Masterpieces of the Oral and Intangible Heritage of Humanity" by UNESCO.

高甲戏

　　高甲戏始于明末清初，其音乐以"泉腔"弦管为主，吸收闽南吹奏乐、笼吹、拾音等艺术之长，唱腔为南音兼收俚歌小调，既有清婉之韵又有刚健之气，语白为闽南方言，角色行当分为生、旦、净、末、丑等种类，尤以丑角表演见长。

　　作为闽南民间喜闻乐见的剧种，现有保留剧目600余个，它主要流传于闽南地区、港、澳以及台湾地区和东南亚华侨聚居地，在海内外有着极大的影响。

　　2006年，高甲戏经国务院批准列入第一批国家级非物质文化遗产名录。

Gaojia Opera

　　Gaojia opera begun in the late Ming Dynasty and early Qing Dynasty. Its music mainly uses string instruments while drawing on the blowing music, Longchui and Shiyin in the South Fujian areas. Its singing includes folk music, gentle but full of energy. Its monologue is the South Fujian dialect. The role includes Sheng (the role of a male actor), Dan (the role of a female actor), Jing (the role of an actor with a painted face), Mo (the role of an old-aged male actor), Chou (the role of a clown) and so on. The act of the Chou is commonly seen.

　　As one of the popular operas in the South Fujian areas, it still has more than six hundred programs. It mainly spreads in the South Fujian areas, Hong Kong, Macao, Taiwan and the gathering place of overseas Chinese in Southeast Asia, which has a great influence both at home and abroad.

　　In 2006, Gaojia Opera was enlisted in the first National Intangible Cultural Heritage List under the approval of the State Council.

歌仔戏

在曾厝垵海边那座圣妈宫里的戏台前，一排一排的长石条凳上，每天都坐满了看戏的人们，戏台上鼓乐悠扬，演着不同的戏码，《陈三五娘》《洛阳桥》《狄青传》《白蛇传》……古人们悲欢离合的故事，用歌仔戏的方式，一代代地演绎着。

歌仔戏是闽南方言的汉族戏曲剧种之一，以流传于闽南的闽南歌仔为基础，吸收梨园戏、北管戏、高甲戏、京剧、闽剧等戏曲之所长而形成。20世纪初，厦门在戴水保等师傅的传授下成立闽南最早的两个歌仔戏班"双珠凤""新女班"。歌仔戏具有浓郁的乡土特色，歌多白少，曲调质朴动人，易于传唱；歌词多为民间语汇，通俗生动。

2006年，歌仔戏经国务院批准列入第一批国家级非物质文化遗产名录。

Gezai Opera

In front of the stage of Shengma Palace beside Zengcuoan beach, rows of stone benches were filled with people coming to watch the Gezai opera. On the stage, with drum and music, there are different Gezai operas every day, including *Chen San and Wu Niang*, *Luoyang Bridge*, *The Legend of Di Qing* and *The Legend of the White Snake*. The sorrows and joys of the ancient people were told through the Gezai opera from generation to generation.

Gezai opera is one of the Han people's operas in Fujian Province. It is sung in the South Fujian dialects. Based on the Gezai popular in South Fujian, it drew from Liyuan opera, Beiguan opera, Gaojia opera, Beijing opera, Fujian opera and so on. In the early 1920s, under the leading of Masters Dai Shuibao and others, there emerged two Gezai troupes in Xiamen, namely, the "Shuangzhu Phoenix Troupe" and the "Xinnv Trope" which were the earliest ones in South Fujian regions. Gezai opera has strong local characteristics with more singing and less saying, plain music and catching rhythm; Most of its lyrics are folk vocabulary, which is popular and vivid.

In 2006, Gezai Opera was enlisted in the first National Intangible Cultural Heritage List under the approval of the State Council.

布袋戏

　　布袋戏是中国传统偶戏中的一种表演形式，它区别于皮偶的皮影戏，与提线木偶同属于傀儡戏的表演形态。因为戏偶的身形如同布袋，又以手掌操弄，因此，布袋戏又俗称"掌中戏""花指戏"，用双手诉说历史。

　　布袋人偶的头是用木头雕刻成中空的人头，除了偶头、戏偶手掌与人偶足部外，布袋戏偶身之躯干与四肢都是用布料做出的服装；演出时，将手套入戏偶的服装中操偶。早期此类型演出的戏偶偶身极像"用布料所做的袋子"，因此有"布袋戏"之通称。

　　2006年，布袋戏经国务院批准列入第一批国家级非物质文化遗产名录。

Glove Puppetry

　　Glove puppetry is a form of the traditional Chinese puppetry act, which is different from the Chinese shadow play. The glove puppetry together with the marionette belongs to puppetry show performance. Because the stature of the puppetry looks like a bag and it is manipulated through the palm, the glove puppetry is also called as "Palm Opera" or "Finger Puppetry". The historic stories are told through the hands.

　　The head of the glove puppet is a hollow man head made of carved wood. Except the head, palms and feet of the puppet, the body and limbs are all made of cloth; when playing, the player will put his hands into the cloth to present the show. In the early days, the body of the puppet looks like a bag made of cloth, so the performance is also called "Glove Puppetry".

　　In 2006, Glove Puppetry was enlisted in the first National Intangible Cultural Heritage List under the approval of the State Council.

答嘴鼓

答嘴鼓是一种喜剧性的闽南方言说唱艺术，表演形式类似于北方的相声，但对白是严格押韵的韵语，语言节奏感很强，流行于闽南地区和台湾地区及东南亚闽南籍华裔聚居地。

答嘴鼓运用丰富多彩、生动活泼、诙谐风趣的闽南方言词语、俚俗语，用闽南方言复杂而富有节奏与音乐美的音韵结构组织韵语，注意情节的敷演与人物的刻画，采用"包袱"的手法与"韦登笑科"（爆笑料）的艺术手段，取得喜剧效果与艺术感染力。

随着现代化进程的加快，人们的生活发生翻天覆地的变化，答嘴鼓通过各种媒体向四方传播，在海外引起强烈反响，成为海外专家、学者研究闽台民俗和语汇的宝贵资料。

2006年，答嘴鼓经国务院批准列入第一批国家级非物质文化遗产名录。

Da Zui Gu

Da Zui Gu is a comic opera belonging to the South Fujian talking-singing art. Its performance form is similar to the cross talk in the north. But its dialogue is strict in rhyme, and has a strong sense of rhythm. It is popular in the South Fujian areas, Taiwan Province and the gathering place of overseas Chinese of South Fujian origin in Southeast Asia.

Da Zui Gu takes advantage of the colorful, vivid, lively, humorous and witty South Fujian dialects as well as complicated and rich rhymes. It also pays attention to the characteristic expression, and adopts both the comic artistic skills and the exaggerating expressions to achieve comic and artistic influence.

With the speeding up of modernization, people's lives undergo great changes. Da Zui Gu is spread through the media and wins popularity abroad. It becomes a precious material for the overseas experts and scholars to study Fujian and Taiwan customs and vocabulary.

In 2006, Da Zui Gu was enlisted in the first National Intangible Cultural Heritage List under the approval of the State Council.

拍胸舞

自宋代以来，拍胸舞就一直在闽南传承着。

拍胸舞传统的舞者为男性，上身裸露、赤足，动作以蹲裆步为主，双手依次拍击胸、胁、腿、掌，配合怡然自得的颠头，并随着舞蹈环境和情绪的变化不同，动作节奏、幅度相应产生不同变化。高昂、激越时可双脚反复顿地，双手使劲将胸、胁、全身拍得通红；舒缓和畅时则抚胸翻掌、扭腰摆臂，动作圆柔而诙谐，活泼而妙趣横生。

拍胸舞强调以身体拍击出声响节奏，一方面体现舞蹈本身的动律特色，一方面也用来协调群体动作，渲染舞蹈气氛，较好地保留了远古闽越舞蹈粗犷、古朴的民族舞蹈遗风。

2006年，拍胸舞经国务院批准列入第一批国家级非物质文化遗产名录。

The Breast-Clapping Dance

Since the Song Dynasty, the breast-clapping dance has been handed down in South Fujian.

The breast-clapping dance is traditionally performed by male dancers, topless and barefoot. They mainly dance squat steps, and they successively beat their chests, flanks, legs and palms with hands, shaking their heads happily. The rhythm and range of steps vary with the change of dancing environment and emotion. With a strong emotion, they will stamp feet repeatedly, clap chest, rib, and the whole body very red with hands; while in a comfortable mood, they will lift chests, turn over palms and twist waists as well as hips, soft and happy, which creates a kind of lively and humorous atmosphere.

The breast-clapping dance emphasizes the rhythm of clapping the body. On the one hand, it reflects the characteristics of the dance itself. On the other hand, it is used to coordinate the group movements and create a kind of dancing atmosphere, well preserving the rugged and simple dance style of traditional ethnic dance of the ancient south of Fujian.

In 2006, The Breast-Clapping Dance was enlisted in the first National Intangible Cultural Heritage List under the approval of the State Council.

4 味蕾 / Delicacy

沙茶面

如果要找出一种最能代表厦门的小吃，非沙茶面莫属。厦门人独创发明了用沙茶酱调制汤底来煮面，日积月累成为名扬四海的厦门小吃。

沙茶始源于马来西亚，也有来自印尼一说。闽南人饮茶成风，因此将马来语的 sate 翻译作闽南语的沙茶 (sa–te)。

沙茶面的做法很简单，碱水油面放入笊篱下开水锅烫熟，捞到碗里，随自己的口味加入猪心、猪肝、猪腰、鸭胗、鸭血、大肠、鲜鱿鱼、豆腐干等辅料，最后淋上一直在大锅里滚开的汤料，一分钟之内一碗面就可上桌了。

Sate Noodles

If you want to find out one of the most representative snacks of Xiamen, it must be sate noodles. People in Xiamen originally modulate the sate sauce as the soup to cook noodles, which gradually has become one of the well–known Xiamen snacks in the world.

Sate originated in Malaysia, but it's also said that it is from Indonesia. The South Fujian people love tea, and thus they transliterated "sate" in Malay into "Sha Cha" (sa–te) in the South Fujian dialect, which literally mean "sand" and "tea" in Chinese.

It is easy to cook sate noodles. First, use colander to put the salt water oil noodles into the boiling water, cook it thoroughly and scoop it into a bowl; then add other ingredients as you like, such as the pork heart, pig's liver, pig's kidney, duck's gizzard, duck's blood, large intestine, fresh squid and dried bean curd; finally, pour the boiling soup in the pot into the noodles. It only takes one minute to cook the sate noodles.

海蛎煎

　　海蛎，又叫蚵仔，绝对是厦门人的碗中宠物。以海蛎为主要原料的海蛎煎是另一道厦门名小吃。

　　海蛎煎选用的是黑耳白肚、个头小小的海蛎珠，味道很是鲜美。拌和青蒜、韭菜、地瓜粉，摊入油锅，两面煎透。讲究一点，还要在入锅后，再摊上打散的蛋液，一道煎熟。起锅时，撒点胡椒，放点香菜，吃时再蘸上芥末、辣酱，好吃得连舌头都要一起吞下去了。

Oyster Omelette

　　Oyster is definitely Xiamen people's favorite food. Oyster omelette with oyster as the main raw material is another well–known Xiamen snack.

　　When cooking oyster omelette, select tiny oysters with black ears and white bellies, which tastes very delicious. Spread the mixture of garlic sprouts, Chinese chives, sweet potato flour into the pan and fry over both sides. If you are a little picky about it, after puting it into the pan, you can spread the beaten egg liquid on it and fry them together. Before the cooking is finished, sprinkle some pepper and put in some Chinese parsley. When you eat, dip it in the mustard and chilli sauce, it will be so delicious that your tongue seems to be swallowed down together.

土笋冻

　　听说过土笋冻的人都会联想起厦门。

　　正宗厦门土笋冻的主原料是一种蠕虫，属于星虫动物门，学名革囊星虫。经过熬煮，虫体所含胶质溶于水中，冷却后即凝结成块状，说得形象一点，就是海鲜做的皮肉冻。

　　吃时浇上调味的酱油、醋、芝麻酱、黄芥末和厦门的蒜蓉辣酱，配以酸甜萝卜、香菜，一股脑塞入嘴里，芥末狂放激越的刺激和土笋冻清冽甘甜的原味及冰凉弹牙的Q感，满嘴的神奇让味蕾得到极大的满足。

面线糊

面线糊，烂而不糊，清而不浊，美味适口，是福建大众化的地方风味小吃。

营养而易消化的面线，加上"以血补血"、能起"食疗"作用的鸭血或猪血，再配上油条，点缀一些葱末、葱头油，色泽黄红青白，一看眼馋，一吃口更馋。尤其秋凉冬寒之际，洒点胡椒粉，吃它一两碗，热乎乎，暖和和，作点心，当早餐，老少咸宜，而且价廉物美口感好。随着生活的提高，饮食进入高层次，面线糊也加料了，可以随个人嗜好，选添小肠、大肠、猪肝、鸭肉、鱼肉，配上油条，真是"鱼与熊掌，皆我所欲"了。

Misua Paste

Misua paste, clear, not overcooked, and delicious, is a popular snack of local flavor in Fujian.

Noodles that are nutrient and easy to digest are matched with duck's blood or pig's blood which can play the role of dietary therapy. With deep-fried dough sticks, green onion, as well as onion oil, the paste looks bright in color and tastes more wonderful and delicious. Especially in the cool autumn and cold winter, you can sprinkle some pepper and eat one or two bowls, hot and warm. It can also be eaten as breakfast dessert, which fits both the young and old people. It is cheap and delicious. As life improves, the diet goes to higher levels. Misua paste also has added ingredients. Therefore, you can follow personal preference to add small intestine, large intestine, pig's liver, duck, fish, and deep-fried dough sticks, which really means you can get what you want.

Sipunculid Worm Jelly

People who have ever heard the sipunculid worm jelly will think of Xiamen.

The main raw material of authentic Xiamen sipunculid worm jelly is a kind of worm which belongs to the sipuncula, and its scientific name is phascolosoma esculenta. After boiling, jellies contained in the body dissolve in the water. After cooling, it condense into blocks. Figuratively speaking, it's meat jelly made of seafood.

When you eat, dip it into the soy sauce, vinegar, sesame paste, mustard as well as Xiamen's chilli garlic sauce, and serve with sweet and sour radish and parsley. Stuff them into your mouth, intense stimulation of mustard, sweet flavor and cold feeling will make your taste bud fully satisfied.

芋包

　　说起美食，老厦门人过年必吃芋包，它的地位类似北方的饺子。但由于加工过程复杂，只有极少数老店才肯做。

　　芋包工序之繁琐，主要是它要用软糯甜香的槟榔芋搓成芋泥为皮，五花肉丁、虾仁、香菇、冬笋干、豆干、荸荠等馅料要分别炒香后包裹进芋皮，再上笼蒸熟。芋包的馅料之复杂、选料之考究，在小吃制作中堪称独一无二，美食总是在精心细心后才妙手而得。

　　刚出笼的芋包，透着热气，清香扑鼻，佐以甜辣酱、芥末、花生酱等味道更佳，品后让人垂涎难忘。

酱油水

　　闽南菜里有一手独到的烹饪手法叫"酱油水"，无论居家还是食肆，酱油水的味道会成为离人的乡愁，也会成为过客的记忆。

　　酱油水的做法很简单，将辣椒、姜、蒜、葱白爆油锅，闻到香味后，依次放入料酒、足够酱油和适量水，无须放盐，烧滚汤汁后放入海鲜就可以了。

Soy Sauce Water

　　In Fujian cuisine, there is a unique cooking technique called "soy sauce water". Whether at home or in the restaurants, the taste of soy sauce water will be the nostalgia for the people, and it will also become travelers' memory.

　　The process of cooking soy sauce water is simple. Put pepper, ginger, garlic, and onion into the pan after the oil is heated. After smelling the aroma, you can successively put cooking wine, enough soy sauce and water. Do not add salt. You need to boil the soup and then add the seafood.

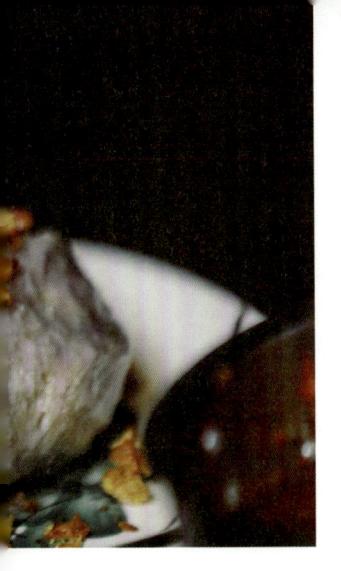

Taro Bun

When it comes to the fine food, old people in Xiamen will always eat taro bun on the Chinese New Year, which is similar to the dumplings in the north. The complicated process of making the taro bun, however, makes it only available in a few old restaurants.

The process of making taro bun is tedious. It uses mashed taro made by soft sweet boilen taros as its wrappers. Its fillings include diced meat, shrimp meat, mushroom, dried bamboo shoots, dried tofu and water chestnuts, which must be separately sauted and then wrapped with smashed taro. The last step is to put it in a steamcage. The ingredients of taro bun are complex and carefully chosen, which is unique in the production of snacks. We can say that fine food is always made by elaboration.

The taro buns which have just come out of the steamer are hot and fragrant. You can add sweet chili sauce, mustard, peanut butter and so on. They will taste better, which is more memorable after tasting.

馅饼

厦门馅饼天下闻名，它是厦门一种具有百年以上历史的传统名点，料精工细，选用优质面粉、猪油、上等绿豆制成。制作时，绿豆蒸酥去壳，研得精细，饼皮和饼酥下足油量，揉得恰到好处。烘制时，注意掌握火候，做到内熟外赤不走油。这样做出来的馅饼饼皮香酥油润，馅料冰凉清甜。

"皮酥馅靓"用来形容厦门馅饼毫不夸张，咬在嘴里，香酥爽口，甜而不腻。

Pie

Xiamen pie is famous all over the world, which is a well-known traditional dessert of Xiamen with a history of more than one hundred years. It is elaborately made of high quality flour, lard and fine mung beans. When cooking pie, you need to steam the mung beans to become crisp, remove their peels, make them fine grinded, put enough oil into the crust and pastry and knead them. When baking, please pay attention to the temperature and make sure pies are well cooked. In this way, the pie crust will be crisp, and the fillings will be cold and sweet.

It's not exaggerated to describe Xiamen pie as having crisp crust and delicious fillings. One bite of it and you will see how it is crisp and refreshing, sweet but not greasy.

同安封肉

从来都说"味浓是故乡",家乡的一道菜、一味小吃就已足够"蛊惑"着四方游子的心。对于同安人来说,一种叫作"封肉"的美食便是他们的心头好。

同安封肉是同安的"三宝"之一,蕴含着丰富的同安文化,是千年古城同安的饮食文化瑰宝。

将猪肉切成四四方方的大块,配上各种佐料:香菇、虾米、板栗等,用北辰山所产的黄栀子叶浸煮的白纱布包裹,如同大印一般,再放入加盖的笼中焖烧而熟,直至上桌才掀开,是以为"封肉"。

每当人们办喜事或建新房,举办筵席,都忘不了"封肉"。侨胞回乡探亲时,也一定要吃这道家乡风味菜。

Tong'an Sealed Meat

It's always said that food from your hometown is the most delicious one. A dish and a snack from hometown is enough to "enchant" the heart of the travelers. For Tong'an people, a kind of food called "Tong'an sealed meat" is their favorite.

As one of the three treasures of Tong'an, Tong'an sealed meat expresses the rich culture of Tong'an, which is regarded as food culture treasures of the old Tong'an with a history of more than one thousand years.

Cut pork into square chunks and serve with a variety of condiments: mushroom, dried shrimps, chestnuts and so on. Wrapped in the gauze which is boiled with the leaves of yellow gardenia jasminoides produced from Beichen mountain, just like a great seal. And then you put it in a covered cage, braised and cooked. Do not open it until you eat it. That is why it is called "sealed meat".

Whenever people hold banquets for wedding or celebrate the building of a new house, they will never forget to eat the sealed meat. When the overseas Chinese return home to visit their relatives, they will also eat this local-flavor dish.

炸五香

厦门有一道美食叫炸五香，将香、酥、脆、鲜都承包了。

它既是小酌佳点，亦是佐餐食品下酒好菜，其味香酥可口，制作较为简便，不少家庭逢年过节都有自行制作炸五香的习惯，在各大餐厅、酒楼或街头小摊也随处可见。

制作炸五香时，将瘦猪肉配上青葱、鳊鱼、荸荠、薯粉、鸭蛋、味精、上等酱油、白糖和五香粉，搅拌均匀，用豆皮包成卷，入油锅炸熟，切成小块；吃时配上沙茶酱、红辣酱、芥末、萝卜酸、香菜、甜酱等佐料，味道可谓鲜美无比。

Fried Ngoh Hiang

Xiamen has a gourmet called fried Ngoh Hiang, which is fragrant, crisp and fresh.

It is not only a delicious dessert, but also a great side dish. It tastes crisp and delicious, and it is simple to make. Many families have the habit of making fried Ngoh Hiang on festivals, and it also can be found everywhere in restaurants or street stalls.

When cooking fried Ngoh Hiang, you need to mix lean pork with scallions, bream, water chestnuts, tapioca, duck egg, aginomoto, soy sauce, sugar and five spice powder. Stir it well, roll it with the bean crust, deep fry it in the pan and cut it into small pieces; When eating it, you can add other condiments such as sate sauce, red chili sauce, mustard, radish, coriander and sweet sauce, and it will taste more delicious.

姜母鸭

　　从姜母鸭这个名字也可以略窥蕴藏其中的闽语特色。"姜母"也就是老姜，在这道菜里又特指三年以上的老姜。俗话说，人老精，姜老辣。三年以上的姜，大概被认为老辣得已经成了精，故称为"姜母"，贴切之中又带有一点市井的俚趣。至于鸭子也有讲究，要选用雄性的正番鸭，据说是这种鸭子的气血刚猛，属于火性强阳之物，配上老姜弥辣之性，有大补元气的功用。

　　取一只粗瓷碗，加少许水，将老姜块茎于碗中研磨，磨出来浓汁，就是上好的调味汁。再将宰杀治净的正番鸭斩成小块，下锅煸干水分，如果食不厌精，还可熬一锅骨头汤，用作煨炖鸭子的汤底。接下来，把煸好的鸭子及姜汁一同倒入汤底，另添入适量的甘蔗、陈皮、黄芪、党参等食材，煨至鸭肉熟烂即可。

Ginger Duck

　　From the name of the ginger (Jiangmu) duck, we can know the hidden features of the Fujian dialect. The Chinese word "Jiangmu" means old ginger. In this dish, it especially means the old ginger that has grown for more than three years. As the saying goes, old people are sophisticated, while old ginger is peppery. Ginger of more than three years is probably considered to be the spiciest, which is also called as "Jiangmu" (the mother of ginger), and the name is appropriate and full of fun. The duck is also specially chosen, which means that you must use male muscovy duck. It is said that this duck is full of nutriments, and can greatly reinforce your energy together with old spicy ginger.

　　You need to grind the ginger in a rough china bowl and put in a little water. After grinding out thick juice, it will be a good sauce. Cut the muscovy duck into small pieces, put them into the pan and make them dried. If you want to eat the finest food, you can boil a pot of bone soup and use it to stew the duck. Next, you put the dried duck and ginger juice into the soup, and add other ingredients properly, such as sugarcane, dried orange peel, astragalus membranaceus and dangshen. Then you stew them until the duck is fully cooked.

FIVE

创新活力
INNOVATION AND VITALITY

厦门,这里充盈**创新活力**,艺文纵横在包容并蓄与锐意开放中弄潮澎湃。

A metropolis of creativity and vitality, Xiamen has become a leader in inclusivity, opening up for arts and literature.

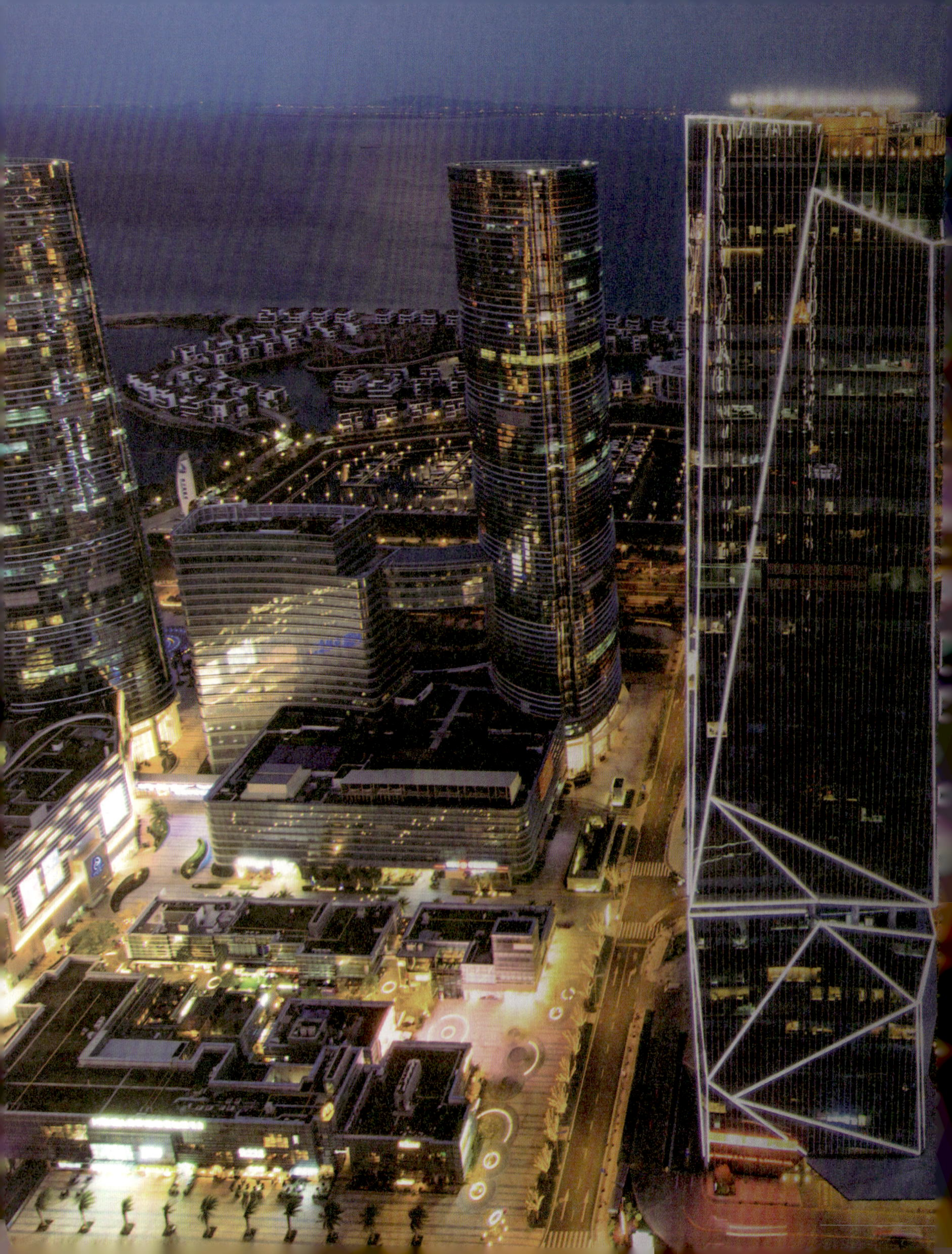

天风行吟,海涛赋诗,厦门是一座属于诗歌的城市。"海外青山山外海,凭高纵目气增豪",清代诗人黄日纪将厦门得天独厚的地理位置描绘得淋漓尽致;"虫沙猿鹤有时尽,正气觥觥不可淘",蔡元培的一首七言绝句让厦门的城市底蕴越发深邃;"凤凰木开花红了一城,木棉树开花红了半空",郭小川的《赞厦门》让厦门的宜居形象跃然纸上……正如诗歌有万千形态,万般情感,厦门这座城也有着千种姿态。

这样一座胸中藏海的英雄城市,能对自己未来命运走向准确把握;这样一座敢闯敢试的先锋城市,有着自觉置身于改革开放风口浪尖前沿的使命担当。厦门,共和国大厦之门,拥有"经济特区、自贸区、自创区、海丝核心区、综改试验区"等多区叠加优势,让我们一起走进她,感受她的锐意进取,体验她的创新活力。

The sound of wind and wave is like singing and composing poems. Xiamen is a poetic city. "The sea is connected with the mountains, and the wide vision makes the mind open", described by Huang Riji, a poet of Qing Dynasty, who portrayed the exceptional advantages of the geographical location incisively and vividly; "Many soldiers died in the wars, but their heroic righteousness would always spread", says a seven-word poem of Cai Yuanpei, which showed the profound deposits of Xiamen; "Delonix regia tints the city red and bombaxes dye the sky red." Guo Xiaochuan's *Praise of Xiamen* demonstrates Xiamen as a livable city. As the poetry has thousands of forms and emotions, Xiamen also has thousands of styles.

This heroic city bearing a maritime dream can grasp its fate precisely. This pioneering city has the consciousness of taking the responsibility to stand at the frontier of the Reform and Opening Up. As the great gate of the People's Republic of China, Xiamen enjoys the overlay advantages of "special economic zone, pilot free trade zone, self-independent innovation area, core area of the Maritime Silk Road, synthetically reform testing district" and so forth. Let's draw close to it and feel its determination, advancement, and experience its innovation and vitality.

1 / 开放
Openness

航空

厦门高崎国际机场，这个最初从动工兴建至正式通航，前后仅用了一年零九个月的机场，已逐步建设成我国重要的口岸机场，也是东南沿海重要的区域性航空枢纽。

出入机场的人群越是川流不息，城市的发展越是蓬勃向上。2019年全年，厦门机场旅客吞吐量达2741.34万人次，同比增长3.2%，保持平稳增长势头。从2015年开始，厦门机场连续开辟悉尼、墨尔本、温哥华、西雅图、洛杉矶、沙巴航线，并增加阿姆斯特丹航班班次，航线覆盖欧洲、北美洲、大洋洲主要国家，使厦门机场一跃成为国际性中转枢纽机场，让世界与厦门有了联结。

让人期待的是，厦门新机场的建设正在有条不紊地进行中。

Aviation

It took Xiamen Gaoqi International Airport only a year and nine months from the construction to formal operation, which has gradually been China's important port airport, and also an important regional hub of the southeast coastal aviation.

The more people come and go in an endless flow at the airport, the more flourishing the city will be. In 2019, passengers throughput of Xiamen airport reached 27.4134 million, an increase of 3.2% to maintain a steady growth momentum. From the beginning of 2015, Xiamen airport opened Sydney, Melbourne, Vancouver, Seattle, Los Angeles and Sabah routes, and increased the frequency of Amsterdam flight. With routes covering major countries of Europe, North America and Oceania, Xiamen airport becomes an international transit hub airport, and establishes a link between the world and Xiamen.

It is expected that the construction of the new airport in Xiamen is in an orderly manner.

港口

厦门,这座有着 1000 多年的海洋交通、海外贸易历史的城市,是我国东南沿海最早对外开放的港口和福建古代四大港口之一。

放眼现在,厦门港不仅是我国沿海主要港口之一,还是我国综合运输体系的重要枢纽、集装箱运输干线港、东南国际航运中心和对台航运主要口岸,2018 年更是位居世界集装箱港口第 14 名。

厦门港拥有便捷的集疏运网络,公路连接全省路网,并通过 319、324 国道及沈海、厦成高速公路与全国公路网相连;直达码头前沿的铁路专用线通过鹰厦、福厦、厦深、龙厦线与全国铁路网相连。丹麦马士基、地中海航运、法国达飞、中远海运等全球前 20 名航运公司均在厦门港设立了分公司或代表机构,并开通了至世界各主要港口集装箱班轮航线。

2018 年 12 月,福建省发挥"海丝"核心区优势,以厦门港为核心,面向全国打造与中欧班列相得益彰的"丝路海运"品牌,织密"海丝"航线网络,建设陆海内外联动、东西双向互济的对外经贸和物流大通道。目前,"丝路海运"命名航线已有 60 条。

Port

Xiamen is a city with more than 1,000 years of marine traffic and overseas trade history, which is the first opening port of China's southeast coast and one of the four ancient Fujian ports.

At present, Xiamen Port is not only one of the major ports along the coast of China, but also an important hub of China's comprehensive transport system, a trunk line port of container transport, a southeast international shipping center and the main port of Taiwan shipping. In 2018, it has been ranked the 14th among the world's container ports.

Xiamen Port has a convenient collecting and distributing network. Its highway connects to the province's road network and to the national road network via National Highway 319, National Highway 324, Shenyang-Haikou Highway and Xiamen-Chengdu Highway. Moreover, the railway special line to the wharfs connects to the national railway network via Yingtan-Xiamen route, Fuzhou-Xiamen route, Xiamen-Shenzhen route and Longyan-Xiamen route. Top 20 global shipping companies including Danish Maersk Line, Mediterranean Shipping, CMA-CGM, and COSCO Shipping have set up branches or representative offices in Xiamen Port, and opened container liner routes to the world's major ports.

In December 2018, Fujian Province made full use of its advantage as the core area of the "Maritime Silk Road" to build the brand of "Silk Road Maritime", which complemented each other with the China-Europe Railway Express, weaving a tight "Maritime Silk Road" course line network and building a great channel of foreign trade and logistics that links the land and sea and benefits the East and West mutually, with Xiamen Port at its core and facing the whole country. At present, there are already 60 named course lines of the "Silk Road Maritime".

高铁

厦门高铁的发展，一如高铁自身的速度，风驰电掣，牵动着无数人的心。2016 年 3 月，人们还在为厦长渝（厦门—长沙—重庆）高铁计划开工建设而激动；到了 7 月，国家公布了《中长期铁路网规划》，勾画了新时期"八纵八横"高速铁路网的宏大蓝图，厦门是其中一纵一横的重要节点城市，这意味着，从厦门出发，可直达 9 个城市群：京津冀、辽中南、山东半岛、东陇海、长三角、珠三角、北部湾、长江中游、成渝。

纵线"沿海通道"串起前 7 个城市群，始于大连（丹东），终于北海（防城港）。其中福厦客专作为省内第一条时速 350 公里的客运专线，已经全线开工建设，1 小时到福州指日可待。横线即厦渝通道，从厦门出发，途经龙岩—赣州—长沙—常德—张家界—黔江—重庆，它将连接海峡西岸、中南、西南地区，贯通海峡西岸、长江中游、成渝等城市群。

High-Speed Railway

Development of Xiamen high-speed railway is just as the flash speed of itself, affecting countless people. In March 2016, people were excited about the opening construction of the Xiamen – Changsha – Chongqing High-speed Rail Project. In July, China announced the *Medium and Long-Term Railway Network Plan*, which outlined the "eight verticals and eight horizontals" blueprint of the high-speed railway network in the new period. As a crucial junction on one "vertical" and one "horizontal", nine city groups can be reached from Xiamen, including Beijing – Tianjin – Hebei, central and southern Liaoning, Shandong Peninsula, East Longhai, Yangtze River Delta, Pearl River Delta, North Bay, the middle reaches of the Yangtze River, and Chengdu and Chongqing.

"Coastal Channel", as the vertical line, has strung seven city groups together from Dalian (Dandong) to Beihai (Fangchenggang). Thereinto, Fuzhou–Xiamen passenger route has been under construction as the first passenger transport line in the province with a speed of 350 miles per hour. To reach Fuzhou in one hour can be expected soon. The horizontal line refers to Xiamen–Chongqing route, which starts from Xiamen and passes through Longyan – Ganzhou – Changsha – Changde – Zhangjiajie – Qianjiang – Chongqing. It will connect the west bank of the strait, central–southern China and southwest region as well as cut through the west bank of the strait, the middle reaches of the Yangtze River, Chengdu and Chongqing and other city groups.

2 纵横 Transportation

桥梁

"岛内外一体化，交通要先行。"1991年，厦门大桥建成通车，它是中国第一座跨越海峡的公路大桥；1999年，在当时亚洲第一、世界第二的悬浮式钢筋悬索桥——海沧大桥建成通车，它代表着20世纪中国建桥水平的最高成就。2008年，厦门市建成集美大桥、杏林大桥，新增厦门北部进出岛车道14条。在同一时间内修建"两桥一隧"跨海通道，厦门书写了世界城市建设史上的奇迹。这些昂首云天、蜿蜒海上的桥梁，连接了被大海分隔的鹭岛与大陆，打通了这座岛城的血脉与持续发展的永动力。

目前，厦门正开工建设第二东通道、跨东海域通道等规划项目，全力推进"两环八射"快速路网建设，实现"厦门各区紧密互动"的大城市格局，使厦门从一座海岛型城市发展成一座海湾型城市。

Bridge

"For the integration of the inside and outside of the island, traffic is the top priority." In 1991, Xiamen Bridge was opened to traffic, which was the first road bridge across the strait in China. In 1999, the Haicang Bridge was opened to traffic, which was Asia's first and the world's second suspension bridge with floating rebar at the time. It could represent the highest achievement of China's bridge construction in the 20th Century. In 2008, Xiamen City built Jimei Bridge and Xinglin Bridge. At the same time, 14 lanes for entry and exit at the north of Xiamen have been increased. The cross-sea channels "two bridges and one tunnel" that set up in the same period have made a miracle in the history of the world's urban construction. These greatly soaring and magnificently marine-situated bridges have connected the Egret Island and the mainland separated by the sea, which have helped to find the "blood vessels" and sustainable power to the development of this island.

At present, Xiamen is starting to build the second east passage, cross-east-sea channel and other planning projects to promote the "two-ring and eight-shot" rapid road network construction, and achieve a metropolis pattern with "close interactions between districts of Xiamen", turning Xiamen into a bay city from an island city.

海底隧道

　　交通是支撑一个城市发展和经济发展的最重要的基础设施。厦门连接岛内外交通的，除了桥梁，还有隧道。

　　翔安隧道，中国大陆第一条大断面海底隧道，也是厦门市本岛第六条进出岛公路通道，连接了厦门岛和翔安区，全长8.695公里，于2010年4月26日建成通车。双向六车道的翔安隧道兼具公路和城市道路双重功能，它的建成通车首次打开了厦门出岛东通道，与仙岳路、海沧大桥共同构筑起厦门第一东西通道，也使厦门出入岛形成了从海上到海底的全天候立体交通格局。

　　此外，还有在建的海沧隧道，全长7.1公里，其中隧道长6.3公里，跨海域长度为2公里，连接海沧区和湖里区，起于海沧马青路互通，穿越厦门西海域，终于火炬北路处。该项目的建设，将为厦漳泉立体交通网络添上浓重的一笔。

Submarine Tunnel

　　Traffic is the most important infrastructure to support the urban development and the economic development. In addition to bridges, Xiamen can also connect the inside and outside of the island by tunnels.

　　Xiang'an Tunnel is China's first submarine tunnel with large cross-section, which is also the sixth route to access Xiamen Island, connecting the island of Xiamen and Xiang'an District. It has a total length of 8.695 km and has opened to traffic on April 26, 2010. Two-way and Six-lane Xiang'an Tunnel has dual function of a highway and an urban road. Its operation has firstly connected east exit passage of Xiamen, and built Xiamen's first east-west channel together with Xianyue Rd and Haicang Bridge. It also forms the all-weather and three-dimensional exit & entry traffic pattern from the sea to the seabed in Xiamen.

　　In addition, there is Haicang Tunnel under construction with a total length of 7.1 km, the tunnel of which is about 6.3 km long and the cross-sea length is 2 km. It starts from the interchange of Haicang Maqing Road, connects Haicang District and Huli District, travels through the Xiamen western waters and finally ends in the Huoju North Road. The construction of this project will make great contributions to the three-dimensional transport network connecting Xiamen, Zhangzhou and Quanzhou.

地铁

2017年9月，厦门地铁开通体验式运行，这意味着厦门即将步入一个崭新的时代——地铁时代。厦门地铁于2014年4月1日正式动工，中间仅历时1000多天，这样的速度在全国也很少见，"厦门速度"再一次举世瞩目。

事实上，厦门地铁建设以来，不仅在速度上为人称赞，在设计领域、质量安全管控、科学文明施工、交通组织疏导等方面也早就受到国家住建部工程质量安全监管司检查组的肯定。特别是厦门地铁建设过程中对树木采取保护性措施，避免了施工损坏。

截止目前，厦门地铁1号线、2号线已开通运营，3号线、4号线、6号线正在如火如荼地建设中。从厦门北站到镇海路，从嵩屿码头到翔安机场，从海沧马銮湾到同安城区，快速直达的轨道交通网络带来的不仅是巨大的客流，更将进一步提升厦门的城市魅力，汇聚起越来越多的资源。

Metro

On September 2017, Xiamen Metro started its experimental operation, which means that Xiamen was about to enter a new era: the subway era. On April 1, 2014 Xiamen Metro officially started to construct, which only lasted for around 1,000 days. This speed was also rare in the country. "Xiamen speed" once again attracted world attention.

In fact, since the construction of Xiamen metro, it has not only been praised for its speed, but also obtained the confirmation from the Inspection Team of Engineering's Quality and Safety Supervision Department of Ministry of Housing and Urban-Rural Development in terms of the design field, quality and safety control, scientific civilized construction, traffic organization and other aspects. Especially in the construction of Xiamen metro, protective measures have been taken to avoid damage of the trees.

Up to now, the Xiamen Metro Line 1 and Line 2 have been opened for operation, with the construction on Line 3, Line 4 and Line 6 in full swing. From Xiamen North Railway Station to Zhenhai Road, from the Songyu Terminal to Xiang'an Airport, and from Maluan Bay of Haicang to Tong'an District, fast and direct access to the rail network will not only bring a huge passenger flow, but also further enhance the charm of Xiamen City and gather more and more resources.

快速公交系统（BRT）

"BRT 好神奇，居然是在空中跑的。"你若问起游客对厦门的印象，BRT 被提及的频率肯定不低，来到厦门，不乘坐一次 BRT，总感觉会留下一点遗憾。

厦门 BRT，大有来头。2008 年 8 月 31 日，全国首条高架且全程专用的快速公交线路，即 BRT 正式开通运营。它的岛内路段采用全程高架形式，在建设过程和模式创新中创造了"三个全国第一"，即第一个多种形式组合、第一个实施高架桥、第一个一次成网的 BRT。

正是因为实现路权的完全专用，能够保证快速、准点、安全，厦门 BRT 一经开通便深受百姓好评，成为沿线市民出行的首选。

Bus Rapid Transit (BRT)

"BRT is so magic, and it actually runs in the air." If you ask visitors about their impression to Xiamen, BRT will definitely be mentioned quite frequently. Visitors who come to Xiamen will always feel a little regretful without taking BRT.

Xiamen BRT has a great backing. On August 31, 2008, domestic first overhead and full dedicated Bus Rapid Transit line, that is, BRT, officially got into operations. Its routes of island section are all overhead forms, which create three "first in China" in its construction process and model innovation, that is, the first combination of diversified forms, the first overhead bridge, and the first one-time BRT network.

It is precisely because the realization of the dedicated use of the road that it can ensure the speed, punctuality and safety. Xiamen BRT has been well received as the preferred travel route by the public since it went into operation.

自行车道

厦门，自行车，当这两个词连接在一起，给人的第一印象当属环岛路上的双人自行车了。在被誉为中国最美马拉松赛道的环岛路上缓缓骑行，身旁是一片美丽海景，沿途木栈道、沙滩、树林，风景如画，大概每个去过厦门旅游的游客都用这样的方式体验了厦门的美。但其实，厦门的骑行路线远远不止这些。

2017年年初，厦门建成全国首条、世界最长的空中自行车道。两侧1.5米高的白色镂空护栏，在让人不觉得"恐高"之余，也不会对人的视野造成影响，可以一边骑行，一边在空中欣赏沿途景色。

岛内自行车道拿下了世界第一，岛外自行车道也发展得毫不逊色。早在2013年，海沧就建成了岛外首条绿道——海沧湖环湖绿道；而全长约20公里的集美环杏林湾自行车道，则是厦门唯一的海上自行车道。

Cycleway

When the two words "Xiamen" and "bike" get together, the first impression is about a double bike on the Island Ring Blvd, which is known as China's most beautiful marathon track. When riding slowly here, you can be surrounded by a beautiful sea view along with the wooden boardwalk, beaches and trees, which is picturesque. Probably every tourist who travels to Xiamen in this way has experienced the beauty of Xiamen. But in fact, Xiamen's riding routes are far more than that.

At the beginning of 2017, Xiamen built the country's first and the world's longest aerial cycleway. The white hollow guardrails with 1.5 meters high on both sides won't make people "fear of height" or cause any impact on the vision. You can enjoy the scenery along the way in the air while riding.

The island cycleway has won the first in the world, and the cycleway outside the island also develops as well as it. As early as 2013, Haicang District has built the first green road outside the island: lake ring green road of Haicang Lake. While the Xinglin Bay ring cycleway in Jimei District which stretches about 20 km is the only marine cycleway in Xiamen.

3 弄潮 Pioneer

自贸片区

从 2015 年 4 月 21 日挂牌起，厦门自贸片区可谓承载着厦门这座城和厦门人的光荣与梦想。贸易自由、人员进出自由、货币流通自由、货物存储自由、货物进出自由……在这个平台上，创业者把生意做到了全世界，自贸区不仅给老百姓带来购物天堂的种种实惠，对推进厦门深化体制改革、推动对台货物贸易自由、深化两岸经济合作也有着特殊意义。

新，是厦门自贸片区的一大关键词，在这片热土上"改革创新"蔚然成风。大胆试、大胆闯、自主改，简化办事流程、提升审批效率，借助"互联网+"创新突破。5 年来，厦门自贸片区累计推出 416 项创新举措，全国首创 82 项；27 项"厦门经验"获全国推广、占全国的 1/4；5 个"厦门样板"入选"最佳实践案例"、约占全国的 12%；22 项"厦门经验"入选福建自贸试验区 30 个最佳创新举措。创新举措为企业带来了实实在在的改革红利，也为产业发展和营商环境的提升注入了活力。

Xiamen Pilot Free Trade Zone

Since it was listed on April 21st, 2015, the Xiamen Pilot Free Trade Zone has been the carrier of the glory and dreams of the city and its people. Freedom of trade, freedom of staff mobility, freedom of money circulation, freedom of goods storage, and freedom of goods mobility ... In this platform, entrepreneurs can do business in the world. Pilot Free Trade Zone not only brings people all the benefits from this shopping paradise, but also plays a significant role in the promotion of deepening system reform, free trade with Taiwan and strengthening the cross-strait economic cooperation.

"New" is the key word for Xiamen Pilot Free Trade Zone. On this land, "reform and innovation" have become common practice. Bold attempt, brave exploration, and independent change have been made to simplify the work process, improve the efficiency of approval, and make breakthroughs with the "Internet +" innovation. Over the past five years, the Xiamen Pilot Free Trade Zone has launched 416 innovative initiatives, 82 of which are national-pioneering initiatives; 27 "Xiamen experiences" have been promoted nationwide, and 5 "Xiamen models" have entered into the "best practice cases" list, accounting for 1/4 and 12% of the whole country respectively; and 22 "Xiamen experiences" have been selected as 30 best innovative initiatives in Fujian Pilot Free Trade Zone. Innovative initiatives have brought tangible reform dividends to the enterprise, and have also energized the growth of the industry and the business environment.

会展片区

　　厦门会晤、投洽会、城市论坛、金鸡奖、时尚周、海洋周、汽车展、佛事展、茶艺展、美食展、艺术展……金融、社会、时尚、生活、艺术，越来越多的国际化、重磅级的展会来到厦门并生根，海内外的人才、资源蜂拥，厦门人的视野越来越广阔。在厦门成为"中国会展名城"和"著名的会议目的地城市"越来越"国际范儿"的路上，会展片区功不可没。临海而建，有着得天独厚的区位优势，这片数十年前曾经偏僻的渔村盐场、荒凉所在，已经成为厦门环岛地区最成熟、最让人向往的片区之一。会展中心、金融商务中心、星级酒店、剧院、高端社区，为这里注入文化、时尚等新内涵，商务、休闲、购物、居住，如今的会展片区已经化茧成蝶，形成全新的商圈，成为厦门新天地。

Conventions and Exhibitions

　　BRICS Summit, CIFIT, City Forum, Golden Rooster Awards, Fashion Week, Ocean Week, Auto Show, Buddhist Show, Tea Show, Food Fair, and Art Exhibition ... Finance, society, fashion, life, art and more and more international and super exhibitions come to Xiamen and take root here. Talents at home and abroad as well as resources flock here, which bring Xiamen people broader visions. On the way of becoming "China's prominent convention and exhibition city" and "famous conference city", Xiamen is more and more "international". The exhibition area contributes to this a lot. It has been built along the sea, which has a unique geographical advantage. Decades ago, it used to be a remote fishing village, a saltern and a desolate place, but now it has become the most mature and one of the most desirable area of Xiamen. Exhibition center, financial business center, star hotel, theater, and high-end community bring culture, fashion and other new connotations here. Business, leisure, shopping and living have made today's exhibition area break the cocoon and turn into a butterfly, and form a new business district. Thus, it becomes a new world of Xiamen.

火炬高新区

　　星星之火可以燎原，象征着创世、再生和光明的火炬更充满着未来和希望。早在 1991 年，厦门火炬高技术产业开发区就被国务院批准为首批国家级高新区，也是全国三个以"火炬"冠名的国家高新区之一。"发展高科技、实现产业化"，长期以来，"火炬园"以原始创新、集成创新、引进消化吸收再创新为基础，努力实现科技成果的商品化、产业化、国际化，取得又好又快的发展成就。这里也成为让优质人才心生向往的所在，不仅有着吸引人的创新创业软硬件条件，还提供"人才公寓"等人性化设施，为在此奋斗的人才解决后顾之忧。

　　在这里，平板显示、计算机与通信设备、电力电器、软件与信息服务、微电子与集成电路、LED 等六大重点产业，以及生物医药、新材料、新能源、文化创意等新兴特色产业得到蓬勃发展，是福建省第一个年产值过千亿元的开发区。

Torch High-Tech District

　　A single spark can start a prairie fire. The torch, symbolizing the creation of the world, regeneration and light, is full of future and hope. As early as 1991, Xiamen Torch High-Tech Industrial Development District has been approved as the first national high-tech district by the State Council, which is also one of the three national high-tech districts naming with "torch". "Developing high technology to realize the industrialization", since long time ago, "Torch park" makes great efforts to realize the commercialization, industrialization and internationalization of the scientific achievement based on the original innovation, integrated innovation as well as introduction, digestion, absorption and re-innovation, and has achieved fast and good development. It has also become a high-quality center to attract lots of talents, which not only has attractive innovation and entrepreneurship hardware and software conditions, but also provides "talent apartment"" and other humanistic facilities to resolve their worries.

　　Here, six key industries including the flat panel display, computer and communications equipment, electrical appliances, software and information services, microelectronics and integrated circuits and LED, as well as emerging industries like biological medicine, new materials, new energy and cultural and creative industries are booming, which make Fujian the first development zone with an annual output value of over 100 billion yuan.

象屿保税区

到保税区去"扫货",已然成为厦门市民、游客乃至周边城市居民购物的一大优选,箱包、化妆品、食品、日用品、酒类、汽车、服装……国际品牌云集,保税直销模式让人们可以享受到比"海淘"更好的便捷和优惠,不用出国,也无须通过代购,就可以在家门口选购到丰富的进口名品。从1992年成立至今,厦门象屿保税区已经深入厦门经济生活、市民生活,累计设立企业1100家,引进外资8亿美元,实现进出口贸易总额超200亿美元。物流园区、东渡港区、航空港工业与物流园区……随着"海空港保税联动区"规划实施的不断推进,作为西太平洋区域性国际中转港的主要组成部分,保税区是闽西南、闽粤赣区域性航运集散中心,也是海峡两岸货物集散中心,它将继续发挥作用并升级。

Xiangyu Free Trade Zone

To go "shopping spree" in the free trade zone has become a prior choice for the Xiamen residents, tourists and even the residents living in the surrounding cities. Luggage, cosmetics, food, daily necessities, alcohol, cars, and clothing ... international brands gather here.The direct sales model of free trade zone can make people enjoy better convenience and discounts than "overseas online shopping". They can get the rich imported goods at home instead of going abroad or asking for procurement service. Since its establishment in 1992, Xiamen Xiangyu Free Trade Zone has been involved in Xiamen economic life and citizen's life. The total number of enterprises has been 1,100, which introduces 800 million US dollars of foreign capital. The total import and export trade is over 20 billion US dollars. Logistics park, Dongdu port area, airport industry and logistics park ... With the continuous advance about planning and implementation of free trade zone of sea port, free trade zone is the regional shipping distribution center of the southwest Fujian and Fujian–Guangdong–Jinagxi, and cross–strait cargo distribution center as the main component of international transit port at the west Pacific region. It will continue to play its role and keep upgrading.

厦门创新创业园

　　一群群创业者从这里踏上梦想的征程，一批批海内外高科技人才纷至沓来，在创新中一家家企业开花、结果。让全世界潮人都爱不释手的"美图"，最大的中文游戏平台4399，还有三达膜、乾照光电、三维丝环保、清源科技……它们都是业界的佼佼者，它们都有一个相同的起点——厦门创新创业园。园内引进培育创新创业型企业超过1600家，成为众多具有自主知识产权项目、技术创新水平高、产业化前景好的优秀高科技企业飞速成长的乐园。

　　"苗圃（众创空间）+孵化器+加速器"，二十多年来越来越完善的创新孵化和企业培育链条，让这里成为创业者的乐土，数百家中小微科技企业在这里孵化，并成长成"科技小巨人"。

Xiamen Innovative and Entrepreneurial Park

　　Many entrepreneurs set up their business here and many high-tech talents all over the world come in a continuous stream. With innovations, numerous enterprises have been established and operated well. For instance, Meitu, fond by the trend setters around the world, 4399, the largest Chinese game platform, Suntar, Changelight, Savings, Clenery and so forth, they are leading enterprises in Xiamen and even the whole nation. They share the same starting point: Xiamen Innovation and Entrepreneurship Park. More than 1,600 innovative enterprises and start-ups have been introduced and cultivated in the park, which has become a wonderland for the excellent hi-tech enterprises with autonomous intellectual property projects, high technological and innovative levels and promising future of industrialization to develop themselves fast.

　　"Seed Bed (Group Innovation Space) + Incubator +Accelerator" make this place become the wonderland for entrepreneurs. The innovative incubation chain and enterprise cultivation chain have been more and more improved in the recent two decades. Hundreds of medium and small micro-technique enterprises are incubated here and have grown into "scientific and technological giants".

厦门软件园

吉比特在上海交易所挂牌上市，是首家在上交所主板上市的游戏企业；罗普特科技园项目落户厦门，总投资约人民币9.25亿元；邀请阿里鱼平台举办优质IP对接会，全市21个优秀原创动漫IP顺利接入；盈趣科技、凤凰创壹等企业积极布局VR装备和VR集成应用产业；国家健康医疗大数据中心与产业园建设试点工程厦门园区在这里揭牌；二次元发展基金助力漫画、动画、文学、图书、影视、游戏等二次元相关产业……无数优秀企业生根、发展于厦门软件园，"厦门硅谷"不断创造着奇迹。

厦门软件园包括软件园孵化基地（一期）、软件园产业基地（二期）和厦门软件园三期，庞大的总建筑面积使之成为全国最大的软件园之一。在科技部火炬中心公布的43个国家火炬计划软件产业基地综合评价排名中，厦门软件园连续两年排名全国第七，成长性指标蝉联全国第一；同时，园区还获评"2018中国服务外包产业集聚园区""2018中国大数据明星产业园"等荣誉称号。

Xiamen Software Park

G-bits listed on the Shanghai Stock Exchange, which is the first listed game company on the Shanghai Stock Exchange; ROPEOK Park project settled in Xiamen with a total investment of about 925 million yuan; Alifish platform was invited to held high-quality IP docking, and 21 excellent original animation IP of this city ware smoothly accessed; Intretech and OneSoft and other enterprises are actively planning to develop the VR equipment and VR integrated application industry; Pilot projects about big data center of national health medical treatment and industrial park opened here; Fund of quadratic element supported the comic, animation, literature, books, film and television, games and other related industries. Numerous outstanding enterprises took root and developed in Xiamen Software Park. "Xiamen Silicon Valley" continues to create miracles.

Xiamen Software Park includes Software Park Incubation Base (Phase I), Software Park Industrial Base (Phase II) and Xiamen Software Park Phase III. The vast total floor area makes it one of the largest software parks in the country. In the comprehensive evaluation ranking of 43 software industrial bases of the National Torch Program announced by the Torch High Technology Industry Development Center of Ministry of Science & Technology, Xiamen Software Park ranked seventh in the country for two consecutive years, and its growth indicators ranked first in the country in a row. Meanwhile, the Park was also awarded honorary titles such as "2018 China's Service Outsourcing Industry Cluster Park" and "2018 China's Big Data Star Industry Park".

观音山国际商务营运中心

厦门环境最好的商务办公地点，非环海而建的观音山国际商务营运中心莫属，厦门岛东部，国际会展中心旁，与金门岛隔海相望。作为海峡西岸最前排的"CBD"，15栋高层写字楼沿海岸线一字排开，型如鼓起的风帆，书写创业奇迹；特殊的地理位置决定了它承接台湾资本的最前沿，在这里，台湾的知名企业及其管理、营销、结算机构比例较大，台湾引进的项目也能得到优先落地、优先发展。商务营运区、配套生活区、旅游休闲区和山体公园区，丰富、完善、人性化的功能区体现了以人为本、科技创新的精髓，也是高标准、高质量的钻石品质。

Guanyinshan International Business Center

Guanyinshan International Business Center, which was built along the sea, is definitely a business office with the best environment in Xiamen. It is located at the east of Xiamen Island and beside the International Conference and Exhibition Center, and faces Jinmen Island across the sea. As the forefront CBD at the west bank of the strait, 15 high-rise office buildings lined up along the coastline like the wind sail, where the miracle of entrepreneurship is created. Special geographical location determines its forefront place to undertake Taiwan's capital. Here, Taiwan's well-known enterprises and relative management, marketing and clearing institutions have a larger proportion, so Taiwan's introduced projects can also be given priority to develop. Functional areas including business district, supporting living area, tourism and leisure area and mountain park area are rich, inclusive and user-friendly, which not only reflect the people-oriented essence with scientific and technological innovation, but also present the diamond quality with high standard and high quality.

生物医药港

当今社会，发展生物产业和培育生物经济已成全球性的大趋势，生物医药与健康产业是"抓产业""惠民生"的重要举措。以海沧区为核心，大手笔规划建设的"厦门生物医药港"是厦门生物医药与健康产业增长的核心引擎。它是生物医药孵化器，为初创型生物医药企业提供服务；是生物医药中试产业化基地，引进唐传木糖醇、虎标万金油、朝阳河豚毒素等项目，设立闽台诊断试剂产品创新创业园；它是生物医药产业基地，实现"孵化器—中试园区—产业基地"的三个梯次发展。厦门生物医药港数百家生物医药企业聚集，工业产值百亿，培育了一批拥有自主知识产权和知名品牌的龙头骨干企业，重点创新产品不断，涌现多个国家级科研平台，自主创新能力已经达到国内领先层次，多个"厦门造"产品领跑全球。

Biomedical Port

Today, developing bio-industry and biological economy has become a global trend, and bio-medicine and health industry is an important measure to "grasp industry" and "benefit people's livelihood". Taking Haicang District as the core, making great efforts to plan and construct "Xiamen Biomedical Port" is the core engine of the growth of Xiamen bio-medicine and health industry. It is the incubator of bio-medicine, providing services to start-up biomedical enterprises; it is a biomedical pilot industrial base, introducing projects such as Thomson Xylitol, Tiger Balm and Chaoyang Tetrodotoxin, andestablishing Fujian and Taiwan diagnostic reagents products innovation pioneer park; it is a biomedical industrial base to achieve the three-echelon development of "incubator-pilot area-industrial base". Xiamen biomedical port has gathered hundreds of biomedical enterprises with billions of industrial output value, and has cultivated many leading enterprises which possess independent intellectual property rights and well-known brands. As a result, key innovative products have been developed continuously; many national research platforms have emerged; independent innovation capability has reached the leading level in China; many "Xiamen-made" products have led the world.

4 艺文 Arts and Literature

龙山文创园

"漫步在这里时,米兰时尚大师是怎样的心情……"这是龙山文创园内的一段墙体涂鸦,文艺气息迎面扑来。只是当你漫步其中时,又何尝能想到,20世纪八九十年代,龙山片区是机器轰鸣的工业厂房呢?

2009年,思明区针对龙山片区的旧厂房采取"微改造",重新规划后的龙山文创园被定位为特色创意中心,重点引进工业设计、时尚设计等创意设计项目。在地方政府的用心培育下,原本"灰头土脸"的工业厂房,逐渐"蜕变"为充满灵性的创意空间。园区初步集聚原创设计、衣料生产、品牌发布、时尚秀场、资本引入等一系列时尚产业链条。

目前,龙山文创园区已引进一批国内外顶级服装设计师入驻,俨然成为"时尚设计师之家",是厦门打造"中国安特卫普"的摇篮。

Longshan Cultural & Recreational Park

"How do Milan fashion masters feel when wandering here?" This is the graffiti on the wall of Longshan Cultural & Recreational Park, full of ambience of arts and literature. But when you walk in the park, how can you imagine that Longshan District was an industrial plant with whirring machines in the 1980s and 1990s?

In 2009, Siming District took the measure of "micro-reconstruction" towards the old factory in Longshan District. The re-planned Longshan Cultural & Recreational Park was positioned as a creative center, focusing on the introduction of creative design projects such as industrial design and fashion design. Under the cultivation of local government with great efforts, the original "old and dilapidated" industrial plant has been gradually "transformed" into a creative space full of spirituality. The park initially gathered a series of fashion industrial chain including original design, clothing production, brand release, fashion show and capital introduction.

At present, Longshan Cultural & Recreational Park has introduced a number of top domestic and foreign fashion designers, just like the "home of fashion designers". It has become the cradle to build Xiamen into a "Chinese Antwerp".

华美文创园

穿越旧时光，遇见新时尚。走进湖里联发华美空间文创园，一栋栋具有时代感的老厂房让人仿佛走进30年前的工业时代；但跨进秀场、文艺咖啡厅等创意空间，又将你拉回现在，处处涌动着时尚的活力。

于2015年年底正式对外开放的华美空间，由联发集团在华美卷烟厂的基础上投资改造而成，园区用地面积4.2万平方米，建筑面积5.7万平方米，是目前湖里区体量最大的花园式文化创意产业园。"不朽的梵高"感映艺术大展曾在这里华丽亮相。华美空间正逐步成为以时尚文化为核心，以时尚传播、生活体验与创意办公为主，展览发布和公共休闲为辅的文创园区。

Huamei Cultural & Recreational Park

Go through the old times and meet new fashion. Walking into Huli Lianfa Huamei Space Cultural & Recreational Park, you will see many old plants with the sense of times as if in the industrial era 30 years ago. But going through show field, arts café and other creative spaces, you will be pulled back to the real world. Everywhere is filled with the vitality of fashion.

Huamei Space was invested and reconstructed by Lianfa Group based on Huamei Cigarette Factory, and was officially open to the public at the end of 2015. At present, it is the largest garden-like cultural and creative industrial park in Huli District, covering a park area of 42,000 square meters and a construction area of 57,000 square meters. "Immortal Van Gogh" Art Exhibition was once held here. Huamei Space is gradually becoming a cultural & recreational park in which fashion culture is the core, with fashion communication, life experience and creative working as the main part and exhibition, release conference, and public leisure as the supplementary part.

海峡文创园

　　缓步走进位于湖里大道14号的海峡两岸建筑设计文创园，文艺气息扑面而来——浓郁的咖啡香，静静陈列着的艺术设计品，设计者们埋着头，专注地用键盘敲击出一个又一个让人惊喜的创意。

　　2012年，厦华电子的3号、4号厂房变身为海峡两岸建筑设计文化创意产业园。这是省内第一家以建筑设计为核心的文化创意产业园，整合建筑装饰产业链，集合海峡两岸优秀设计师和设计机构，融国际设计艺术家推广、优秀设计师和设计产品推荐及创业设计师孵化于一体。

　　当老厂房遇上文化创意，也就碰撞出别样火花。目前，园区共有近百家优秀设计创意企业入驻。

Haixia Cultural & Recreational Park

　　Walking slowly into the Cross-Strait Architectural Design and Cultural & Recreational Park which is located at the No. 14 Huli Avenue, you will feel the literary and artistic atmosphere. Designers are working hard to produce surprising ideas, accompanied by the fragrance of coffee and the art design quietly displayed on the wall.

　　In 2012, the No. 3 and No. 4 plants of Xiamen Overseas Chinese Electronic Co., Ltd. were reconstructed into Cross-Strait Architectural Design and Cultural & Recreational Park. It is the first cultural and creative industrial park with architectural design as its core in Fujian Province to integrate architectural decoration industrial chain, to collect cross-strait outstanding designers and design agencies, and to integrate the promotion of international design artists, the recommendation of excellent designers and design products and the cultivation of start-up designers.

　　The encounter between old factory and culture and creativity can produce a special spark. At present, the park has about a hundred of outstanding design creative enterprises.

5 澎湃 Surge

2017年金砖国家峰会

　　2017年9月3日，第九次金砖国家峰会在中国厦门举行。"一座高素质的创新创业之城"、"一座高颜值的生态花园之城"，在会晤期间，国家主席习近平面向全世界多次点赞厦门。这座城市被迅速推向世界舞台的"风口"，全球知名度得到了裂变式提升，世界的目光由此聚焦厦门，感受这座城市的独特韵味、别样精彩。

　　回望2006年金砖机制的发轫，长路悠悠，今日的金砖国家已然成为促进世界经济增长、推动全球秩序变革、维护国际和平稳定的关键力量。在见证金砖国家光辉的同时，厦门怀揣着作为中国现代文明城市典范的自信，以中国人特有的文化素养，向世界展示了中国东南滨海城市的风采。成功保障厦门会晤，证明了厦门这座城市的能力与实力。在筹备、举办厦门会晤过程中的好经验好做法好机制，也为厦门市承办更多国际性会议活动、打造国际知名旅游会展城市积累更多经验。

2017 BRICS Summit

　　On September 3, 2017, the 9th BRICS Summit was held in Xiamen, China. "a city of high-quality innovation and entrepreneurship" and "a city of beautiful ecological gardens" – this is how Xi Jinping, President of the People's Republic of China, more than once praised Xiamen to the world during the meeting. The city was quickly brought under the "spotlight" of the world stage, with its global popularity raised in a fission fashion. The world's eyes gathered on Xiamen to feel the unique charm and distinctive splendor of the city.

　　Tracing back at the commencement of BRICS mechanism in 2006, a long way has been passed. The BRICS countries today have become a key force to drive up world economic growth, promote global order transformation and maintain international peace and stability. While witnessing the glory of the BRICS countries, Xiamen holds the self-confidence as a model of China's modern civilized cities and shows the elegance of China's southeast coastal cities to the world, with the unique cultural qualities of the Chinese. Successfully guaranteeing this meeting in Xiamen proves Xiamen's ability and strength. The good experience, practice and mechanism during the preparation and holding of the Summit in Xiamen also provide more experience for Xiamen to host more international conferences and activities and build an internationally famed city of tourism, convention and exhibition.

中国国际投资贸易洽谈会

中国国际投资贸易洽谈会（简称"投洽会"）经中华人民共和国国务院批准，于每年9月8日至11日在中国厦门举办。届时相关国家领导人、国际经济组织负责人、专家学者、企业家等人都会莅会演讲，每一年都是国内外瞩目的大事件。

投洽会以"引进来"和"走出去"为主题，以"突出全国性和国际性，突出投资洽谈和投资政策宣传，突出国家区域经济协调发展，突出对台经贸交流"为主要特色，是中国目前唯一以促进双向投资为目的的国际投资促进活动，也是通过国际展览业协会（UFI）认证的全球规模最大的投资性展览会，主要内容包括：投资和贸易展览、国际投资论坛及系列投资热点问题研讨会和以项目对接会为载体的投资洽谈。

多年来，投洽会努力顺应国内外经济形势变化，适时调整办会主题和内容，逐步从最初的区域性经贸活动发展成为当今全球最具影响力的国际投资促进盛会。

China International Fair for Investment and Trade

China International Fair for Investment and Trade (referred to CIFIT), approved by the State Council of the People's Republic of China, takes place on September 8 to 11 every year in Xiamen, China. Relevant state leaders, heads of international economic organizations, experts and scholars and entrepreneurs will attend the fair and deliver their speeches. CIFIT is a big event attracting tremendous attention at home and abroad every year.

Themed on "Introducing FDI" and "Going Global", CIFIT "focuses on nationality and internationality, investment negotiation and investment policy promotion, coordinated development of national and regional economy, as well as economic and trade exchanges across the Taiwan Strait". CIFIT is currently China's only international investment promotion event aimed at facilitating bilateral investment. It's also the largest global investment fair approved by the Global Association of the Exhibition Industry (UFI). CIFIT has the following major components: investment and trade exhibition, the International Investment Forum (IIF), a series of seminars on hot investment issues, and investment project matchmaking symposia.

Over the years, in response to the changes in economic situation at home and abroad, CIFIT has timely adjusted its theme and contents, and has gradually developed into one of the most prestigious international investment expositions from a regional economic and trade event.

厦门马拉松赛

湛蓝如洗的天际线,绿树掩映的赛道,如花似锦的环岛路变身欢腾的海洋。随着发令枪响,万头攒动的人群,一路向前,动力不减,在赛道上快乐驰骋。

截至2020年年初,创办于2003年的厦门马拉松赛已成功举办18届,自2008年起,连续13年荣获"国际田联路跑金标赛事"认证。十多年来,厦门马拉松早已成为厦门市民的狂欢盛会,一场竞技体育赛事在这里变成全民体育赛事,成为经济推手、环保公益汇集的代名词。

2017年的厦门马拉松作为元旦后中国境内第一场金标比赛,首次升级为"全马"赛事,成为继北京马拉松后的全国第二大"全马"赛事,邀请来自世界不同国家的数十名优秀运动员参赛。随着中国马拉松博览会落户厦门、"全球马拉松第一跑"的开跑,这座城市再次向世界展示多元和国际化的城市风采。

Xiamen Marathon

The beautiful Island Ring Blvd looks like the sea of jubilation with the cloudless blue sky and the track surrounded by green trees. As the starting gun goes off, thousands of competitors full of energy happily run forward on the track.

As of the beginning of 2020, Xiamen Marathon, founded in 2003, has been successfully held for successive 18 sessions. Since 2008, this marathon has won the "Association of International Marathons and Distance Races (AIMS) & International Association of Athletics Federations (IAAF) Gold Medal Race" for 13 years. For more than a decade, Xiamen International Marathon has become a carnival event for Xiamen people. An athletic sporting event has become a sporting event for all and become the synonym of the economic promoter and integration of environmental protection and public welfare.

In 2017, the Xiamen Marathon, the first gold medal race in China after New Year's Day, was upgraded to a full marathon for the first time, making it the second largest full marathon after the Beijing Marathon. Dozens of excellent athletes from all over the world were invited to participate. With the China Marathon Expo held in Xiamen and the beginning of "Global Marathon First Running", this city showed its urban style of diversity and internationality to the world.

海峡两岸（厦门）文化产业博览交易会

海峡两岸（厦门）文化产业博览交易会（以下简称"海峡两岸文博会"）是中国大陆唯一以"海峡两岸"命名并由海峡两岸共同主办的综合性文化产业博览交易会，以"一脉传承·创意未来"为主题，以"突出两岸、突出产业、突出投资、突出交易"为宗旨，以促进两岸文化交流为目的，推动两岸文创产业的合作和落地。

经过12年的培育与发展，海峡两岸文博会形成了较为成熟的工艺艺术品、创意设计、数字内容与影视、文创旅游四大专业板块格局，发展成为两岸文化产业交流合作与投资交易的重要平台。

Cross-Strait (Xiamen) Cultural Industries Fair

Cross-Strait (Xiamen) Cultural Industries Fair (hereinafter referred to as "Cross-Strait Cultural Industries Fair") is an unique integrated "cross-strait" cultural industries fair in Mainland China co-hosted by the cross-straits, which aims at boosting cooperation and implementation of cross-strait creative industries, with the theme of "Same Lineage & Creative Future", the tenet of "focusing on cross-straits, focusing on industries, focusing on investment, focusing on trading" and the purpose of promoting cross-strait cultural exchange.

Through 12 years of cultivation and development, the Cross-Strait Cultural Industries Fair has formed relatively-mature sectors: craft art, creative design, digital contents and films and televisions, and cultural and creative tourism, and has become an important platform for exchange, cooperation, investment and trading of cross-strait cultural industries.

海峡论坛

　　海峡论坛是在已举办三届的"海西论坛"基础上发展扩大并更名的。首届海峡论坛于2009年5月15日至22日在福建省厦门、福州、泉州、莆田等地隆重举行。2019年6月15日，第十一届海峡论坛在厦门拉开帷幕，论坛延续"扩大民间交流、深化融合发展"主题，聚焦基层民众和青年群体，安排青年交流、基层交流、文化交流、经济交流四大板块67场活动，由大陆41家、台湾42家共83家两岸单位共同主办，台湾各界人士10000余人出席。

　　从2009年创办至2019年，海峡论坛已步入第十一个年头。十一年来，海峡论坛始终秉持"两岸一家亲"理念，面向青年、面向基层，民间性、广泛性特色鲜明；十一年来，海峡论坛每年都吸引上万名两岸基层民众和各界人士参加，大家共叙亲情乡情，共谋民生福祉，共圆复兴之梦，极大地促进了两岸同胞的情感交融和心灵契合。

Strait Forum

　　The Strait Forum is developed and renamed on the basis of the "Haixi Forum" which has been held for three times. The first Strait Forum was held in Xiamen, Fuzhou, Quanzhou and Putian in Fujian Province from May 15 to 22, 2009. On June 15, 2019, the 11th Strait Forum kicked off in Xiamen. The theme of "expanding non-governmental exchanges, deepening integrative development" was continued for the forum, focusing on the communities and youth groups and arranging 67 activities of four major sectors – youth exchanges, communities exchanges, cultural exchanges and economic exchanges. It was co-hosted by 83 cross-strait units (41 from the mainland and 42 from Taiwan) with more than 10,000 people from all walks of life in Taiwan attending it.

　　Since its set-up in 2009 to 2019, the Strait Forum has entered its eleventh year. In the past eleven years, the Strait Forum has always adhered to the idea of "Compatriots from Both Sides of the Taiwan Strait are of One Family" and been oriented to the youth and the communities with distinctive nongovernmental and extensive characteristics. In the past eleven years, the Strait Forum has attracted tens of thousands of populace from communities and people from all sectors from both sides of the Strait to participate. People sit together to talk about their passion for the family and the hometown, to make contributions to people's welfare and to fulfill the dream of rejuvenation, which has greatly promoted the emotional integration and spiritual consonance of compatriots from both sides of the Strait.

中国厦门国际石材展览会

大理石造的豪车、先进雕刻仪器在石头上"画画"……每一年，中国厦门国际石材展上都会汇聚新鲜、有趣的新技术及形形色色的石头，让人大饱眼福。

中国厦门国际石材展自2001年创办以来，充分利用闽南石材产业和厦门港口优势，在各主办、承办单位的共同努力下，迅速发展壮大，并一举成为全球展览规模最大、参展企业数最多的专业石材展览会。

展会的成功举办，使厦门及周边地区石材企业及时全面地掌握了全球石材资源开采、技术装备、产品设计和应用开发的现状及发展动态的整体水平，缩小了与国际的差距，并使厦门成为辐射全球石材行业的"国际石材中心"，促进了闽南经济持续蓬勃发展和会展业的进步。

China Xiamen International Stone Fair

Every year, there will be new and interesting technology and all kinds of stones on China Xiamen International Stone Fair, such as luxury cars made of marble stone and advanced carving instruments "painting" on stones, which is a feast for people's eyes.

Since its founding in 2001, China Xiamen International Stone Fair has developed rapidly and become a professional stone exhibition with the largest exhibition scale and the largest number of exhibitors in the world after making full use of the advantages of the South Fujian stone industry and Xiamen port under the joint efforts of the organizers and sponsors.

The success of the fair makes the stone enterprises of Xiamen and surrounding areas timely and comprehensively informed of the current situation and the overall level of development of global stone resources mining, technology and equipment, product design and application development, which narrows the gap between Xiamen and the international stone industry. It also makes Xiamen the "international stone center" which influences the global stone industry, and has promoted the sustainable development of southern Fujian economy and the progress of the exhibition industry.

中国金鸡百花电影节

中国电影金鸡奖创办于1981年,金鸡奖评奖委员会是由中国最具权威的导演、表演艺术家、电影剧作家、摄影家、音乐家、美术家,以及电影理论家、教育家、事业家共同组成。金鸡奖与中国电影华表奖、大众电影百花奖并称为"中国电影三大奖",也与香港电影金像奖、台湾电影金马奖并称为"华语三大电影奖"。

2019年4月9日,中国金鸡百花电影节(金鸡奖年份)落户厦门新闻发布会举行。会上宣布,从2019年开始,金鸡奖将长期落户厦门,这也是金鸡奖首次长驻一个城市。

2019年11月19日–23日,第28届中国金鸡百花电影节在厦门举办。600多位老中青三代中国电影人,在厦门这座先锋之城,用一场场论坛、一部部电影,致敬伟大新时代,吹响中国电影再出发的号角。

China Golden Rooster and Hundred Flowers Film Festival

The China Golden Rooster Awards was founded in 1981. The Golden Rooster Awards Committee is composed of the most authoritative directors, performance artists, screenwriters, photographers, musicians, artists, film theorists, educators and entrepreneurs in China. The Golden Rooster Awards, together with the Ornamental Column Awards and the Hundred Flowers Awards, are known as "Three Grand Awards for Chinese movies" and together with Hong Kong Film Awards and Taiwan Golden Horse Awards, are known as "Chinese Three Big Movie Awards".

On April 9, 2019, the press conference of the China Golden Rooster and Hundred Flowers Film Festival (the Golden Rooster Awards Year) settling in Xiamen was held. On the conference, it was announced that the Golden Rooster Awards would be settled in Xiamen for a long time since 2019, which was the first time that the Golden Rooster Awards would be settled in a city for long years.

From November 19 to 23, 2019, the 28th China Golden Rooster and Hundred Flowers Film Festival was held in Xiamen. More than 600 Chinese filmmakers, from three generations of old, middle-aged and young, gathered in Xiamen, the City of pioneers, to salute to the great new era and sound the clarion call for the new starting point of China's films industry with forums and films.

厦门国际海洋周

自 2005 年创办以来，厦门国际海洋周已发展成为一个公众广泛参与的海洋文化节日，一个全球海洋政策、科学技术、决策和行动的交流平台。

截至 2019 年，已经走过十三载春秋的厦门国际海洋周，已成为 14 个重要的海洋国际组织联合参与主协办的全球性海洋盛会，成为与瑞典斯德哥尔摩"世界水周"相媲美的世界唯一的海洋周，成为中国与世界海洋界交流的一大重要平台。海洋周的发展壮大，也正是厦门努力打造具有竞争力海洋强市的一个缩影。

World Ocean Week in Xiamen

Since its set-up in 2005, the World Ocean Week in Xiamen has been developed into an ocean cultural festival with extensive public participation and a communication platform for global ocean policies, science and technology, decisions and action.

Till 2019, the World Ocean Week in Xiamen which had a history of 13 years has become a global ocean event jointly organized by 14 important ocean international organizations, the only ocean week in the world comparable to the "World Water Week" of Stockholm, Sweden and an important platform for communication between China and the world ocean circles. The development and expansion of the Ocean Week is also a microcosm of Xiamen's efforts to build an ocean city with strong competitiveness.

鼓浪屿钢琴节

在鼓浪屿的历史中，钢琴一直是不可或缺的文化符号。

钢琴之岛是对鼓浪屿的礼赞，鼓浪屿钢琴节是对那美好过往的传承与发展。自 2002 年首办以来，钢琴节历经 18 年，已成功举办九届，成为琴岛一块亮丽的音乐品牌，是琴岛为全世界献上的公益性的世界高水平音乐艺术盛宴。

Gulangyu Piano Festival

In the history of Gulangyu Island, piano has always been an indispensable cultural symbol.

The island of piano is a praise for Gulangyu, and the Gulangyu Piano Festival is the inheritance and development of the beautiful past. Since the first holding in 2002, the festival has been successfully held for nine sessions within 18 years. It has become a great music brand of the piano island, and the non-profit music art feast of a high level for the world.

SIX

诗意栖居
POETIC LIVING

厦门，这里安享**诗意栖居**，乐学宜居在**博物开卷**中生长闲趣与流韵。

A place where poetic living is enjoyed, Xiamen is home for happy learning and leisurely living in abundant resources.

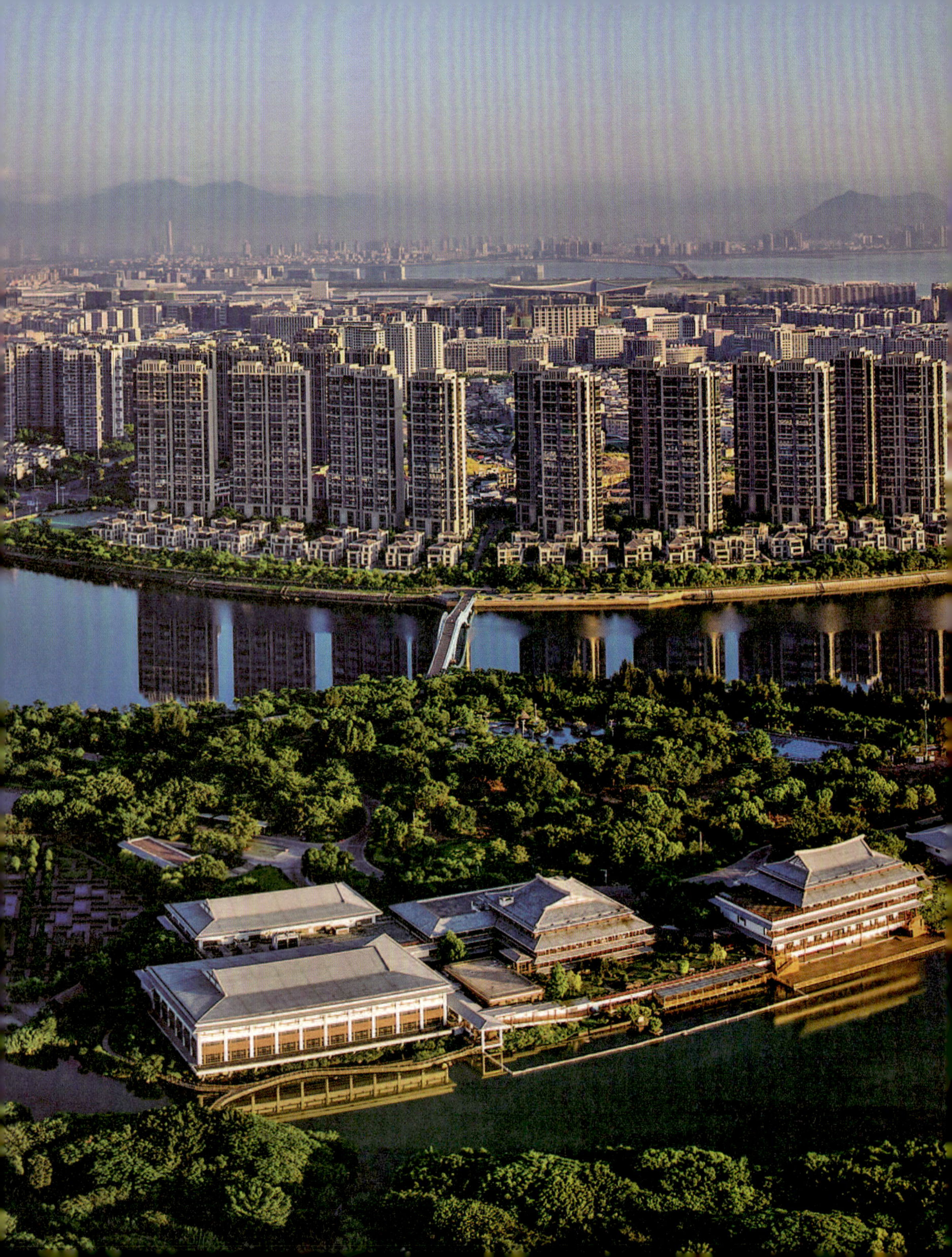

"厦门岛很美很美。

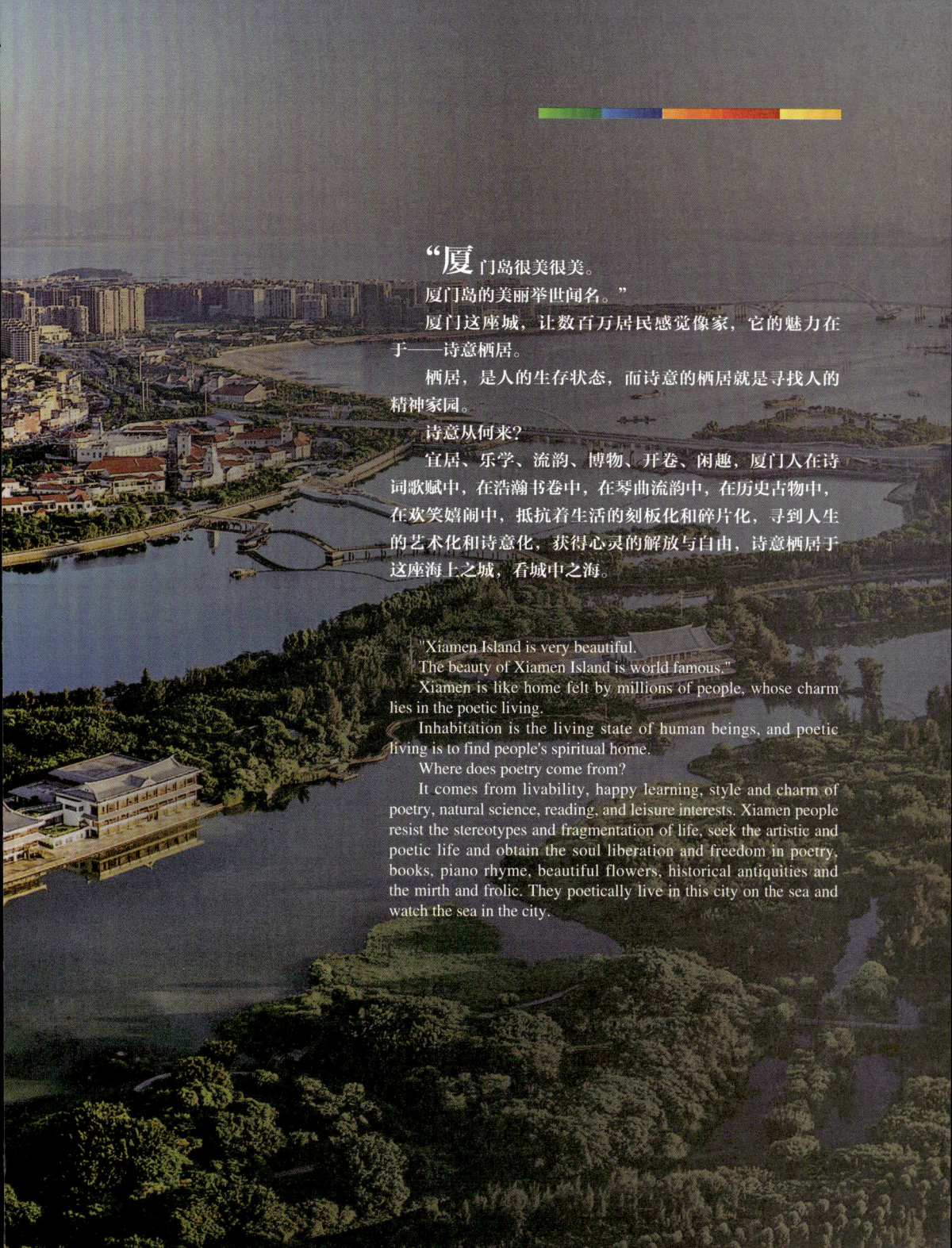

厦门岛的美丽举世闻名。"

厦门这座城,让数百万居民感觉像家,它的魅力在于——诗意栖居。

栖居,是人的生存状态,而诗意的栖居就是寻找人的精神家园。

诗意从何来?

宜居、乐学、流韵、博物、开卷、闲趣,厦门人在诗词歌赋中,在浩瀚书卷中,在琴曲流韵中,在历史古物中,在欢笑嬉闹中,抵抗着生活的刻板化和碎片化,寻到人生的艺术化和诗意化,获得心灵的解放与自由,诗意栖居于这座海上之城,看城中之海。

"Xiamen Island is very beautiful.
The beauty of Xiamen Island is world famous."

Xiamen is like home felt by millions of people, whose charm lies in the poetic living.

Inhabitation is the living state of human beings, and poetic living is to find people's spiritual home.

Where does poetry come from?

It comes from livability, happy learning, style and charm of poetry, natural science, reading, and leisure interests. Xiamen people resist the stereotypes and fragmentation of life, seek the artistic and poetic life and obtain the soul liberation and freedom in poetry, books, piano rhyme, beautiful flowers, historical antiquities and the mirth and frolic. They poetically live in this city on the sea and watch the sea in the city.

1 宜居
Leisurely Living

社区治理

美丽厦门的一个个美丽社区，成为全国社区治理创新的样本，这座城市被民政部确定为"全国社区治理和服务创新实验区"。

官任社区，来自46个国家和地区的1400多名外籍人士居住于此，各种肤色的朋友平安和谐地在一起，这里是个"联合国"大家庭。

兴隆社区，这里生活着一群可爱并乐于奉献的"台湾新住民"，每天上演着"两岸一家亲""血浓于水"的温情故事，这里是厦门台胞台商居住、创业的聚集地。

兴旺社区，这里先行先试，成立了全市首个社企同驻共建理事会，组建了合唱团、俱乐部、义工队等社会组织，社区居民和企业共建、共管，这里是厦门推行新社区治理模式的典型示范区。

厦门，以民生需求为导向，以社区减负为突破口，以完善社区建设为基础，初步探索了一套社区治理创新体系。

Community Governance

The beautiful communities of beautiful Xiamen have become the models of innovative community governance across China. This city has been designated as the "national community governance and service innovation experimental zone" by the Ministry of Civil Affairs.

Guanren Community is a "united nations" family where more than 1400 foreigners from 46 countries and regions in different skin colors live in harmony.

Xinglong Community is the gathering place for Taiwan compatriots and Taiwan businessmen living and starting business in Xiamen, where a group of "Taiwan new residents" who are lovely and willing to contribute live and vivify the warm story of "both sides of the Taiwan Strait belong to the same family" and "blood is thicker than water".

Xingwang Community is the typical demonstration area where Xiamen has implemented the new community governance mode, where there is the city's first council co-built and co-constituted by the society and enterprises, and social organizations such as choir, clubs and volunteer groups, all of which are co-built and co-managed by the community residents and enterprises.

Xiamen has initially developed a set of community governance innovation system by taking the needs of people's livelihood as the guide, the reduction of community burden as the main goal and the improvement of community construction as the basis.

医疗卫生

厦门深化医药卫生体制改革，以破解群众看病难、看病贵问题为目标，按照"标准提高、时间提前、特色突出"要求，充分体现厦门特色，创全国医改典范城市。

强调公立医院的"公益性"和"协同改革"，通过差别化的财政补偿和投资机制、差别化的医保支付政策、打造智慧医疗体系等，为厦门医改提供全面的政策支持。

构建分级诊疗体系，慢性病和普通门诊下基层，实现"让医院放得下、社区接得住、病人愿意去、疾病治得好"，最终构建起双向转诊制度，适当减少三级医院普通门诊；基层医疗卫生机构转诊，上级医院优先接诊；专家门诊较大比例号源用于基层医疗卫生机构转诊；完善康复病人、慢性病人等下转基层条件及程序。

Medical and Health Care

Xiamen has deepened the reform of medical and health care system in accordance with the requirements of "raising the standard, reducing the time and highlighting the characteristics", aimed at solving the problem that it is difficult and expensive to see a doctor for the masses, so as to fully embody the characteristics of Xiamen and build a national model city in medical and health care reform.

The "public interest" and "coordinated reform" of public hospitals should be emphasized. Differentiated financial compensation and investment mechanism, differentiated medical insurance payment policy and the construction of a intelligent medical system should be completed to provide comprehensive policy support for Xiamen medical and health care reform.

Xiamen is committed to building a hierarchical medical system, and chronic diseases and general out-patient service are conducted in basic hospitals, so as to realize the aim "that hospitals can hold, communities can receive, patients are willing to go and diseases can be cured". Therefore, Xiamen can finally construct a two-way referral system and properly reduce general service of tertiary hospitals, and realize referral between primary healthcare institutions and new patients are firstly received in superior hospitals. A large proportion of appointment numbers of specialist clinic will be used to referral in primary healthcare institutions. The conditions and procedures for convalescent patients and chronic patients to be transferred to basic hospitals will be improved.

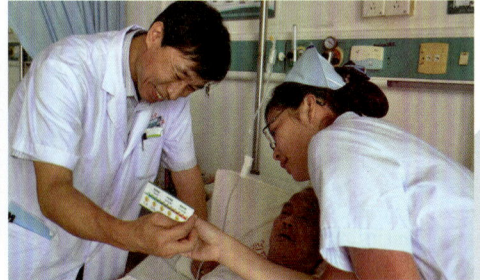

社会保障

厦门市的社会保障力度正不断加大。据厦门政府工作报告显示，2019年厦门新增就业26.18万人，城镇登记失业率控制在4%以内；同时，为5.34万家企业发放稳岗补贴1.68亿元。近年来，厦门市基本养老、基本医疗、工伤、失业、生育五项保险参保人数增长较快，企业退休人员月平均养老金提高到3526元，城乡低保标准提高到每人每月800元。目前，厦门市正加快爱心护理院扩建工程及爱鹭老年养护中心的建设，实现居家养老服务全覆盖，让市民"老有所养、老有所依"，并获批国家医养结合试点城市。

Social Security

The coverage of Xiamen social security has been increasingly expanded. According to the Xiamen government work report, Xiamen has created 261,800 jobs in 2019, and the urban registered unemployment rate was kept within 4%. Besides, it subsidized 168 million yuan for stabilizing employment to 53,400 enterprises. In recent years, the number of persons participating in basic endowment insurance, basic medical insurance, employment injury insurance, employment insurance and maternity insurance of Xiamen has been increased rapidly. The average monthly pension of corporate retirees reached 3,526 yuan, and the standard for urban and rural subsistence allowances was increased to 800 yuan per person per month. At present, Xiamen is accelerating the expansion project of the nursing homes and the construction of Ailu elderly nursing centers, so as to achieve the full coverage of home-based care services, and "make the old people be taken care of with a sense of security". It has been approved as the national pilot city with combined medical and care services for the elderly.

住房保障

"房子是用来住的，不是用来炒的。"多年来，厦门城市决策者和管理者一直把让老百姓住有所居作为重要目标，在住宅市场化的不同阶段采用不同方式，逐步解决居民的住房困难问题，构建起厦门立体式多渠道的住房保障网。首先，厦门市不断加大力度推进保障性住房建设与分配，打造保障性住房的"厦门蓝本"，基本实现了低保家庭的应保尽保。其次，考虑到面对日益高起的房价，许多来厦创新创业的新市民，难免望房兴叹，厦门又于2016年推出面向"夹心层"及稳定就业新市民等更广泛群体的公共租赁住房，着力为其提供更为稳定的居所。

2017年，厦门市推出"地铁站点+保障性住房"，在岛外翔安、同安、海沧、集美四区各选址一处建保障房地铁社区，这是厦门借鉴香港等城市建设的成功经验，将保障房这一住房民生保障工程与地铁大运量交通相结合的创新模式。目前，翔安新店、同安祥平和海沧马銮湾等三个保障房地铁社区一期项目已相继封顶，力争2020年全部交付使用。

House Security

"Houses are built for living, not for speculation." For many years, the city decision-makers and officials in Xiamen always put "ensure that all our people enjoy their rights to housing" as their final goal. They take different measures during different stages of the marketization of houses in order to solve the housing difficulties for the people. They establish a housing security network which is three-dimensional and multi-channel. First of all, the Xiamen government makes great efforts to promote the construction and distribution of indemnificatory housing to build the "Xiamen Example" for indemnificatory housing. Thus, the need of the household receiving subsistence allowances is basically met. Secondly, the price of the houses continues to rise day by day, which leads to the situation that many new citizens who come to Xiamen for jobs can't afford these houses. Therefore, in 2016, Xiamen government built up many public renting houses for those who are not qualified to apply indemnificatory housing and cannot afford to buy an ordinary residential house, and new citizens who want to have a stable job here, aiming at providing them with more stable living places.

In 2017, Xiamen City launched "metro station + indemnificatory housing" policy to build a metro community of indemnificatory housing respectively in the four districts of Xiang'an, Tong'an, Haicang and Jimei. This is an innovative mode adopted by Xiamen, introducing the successful experience of urban construction like Hong Kong and combining the livelihood security housing project of indemnificatory housing, and the mass transit of metro. At present, the first phase of the three metro communities of indemnificatory housing in Xiang'an Xindian, Tong'an Xiangping and Haicang Maluan Bay has been capped in succession, striving to fully deliver the communities for use by 2020.

乡村振兴

天蓝，地绿，水净，民富。

岛内岛外，渔村田野，一座座漂亮别致的小楼掩映在绿树丛中，一条条洁净的水泥路环绕着村庄，一片片四季常青的绿地点缀在房前屋后。

2018年厦门市委农村工作会议上传递出新的声音：让农业成为有奔头的产业，让农民成为有吸引力的职业，让农村成为安居乐业的美丽家园。厦门开启了全面深化农村改革，深入实施乡村振兴战略的征程。今天，厦门乡村振兴交出了一张优异的成绩单——都市现代农业、现代化美丽乡村建设、乡村创新治理等方面多点开花，"三农"经济数字不断刷新，人民的收入水平再上新台阶。

村庄秀美，环境优美，生活甜美，社会和美。这是厦漳泉交界处军营村梯田式的茶园，这是大宅村的火龙果、前格村的菊花田……朝着"产业兴旺、生态宜居、乡风文明、治理有效、生活富裕"的美丽蓝图，乡村振兴，正逐渐从梦想照进现实。

村美城新，发展中的鹭岛，将建设的号角吹响在小城镇中。一座座新城规划兴建，一条条道路拓开新径，一个个民生项目拔地而起。新城的建设，为农村人打开了世界的窗口，城镇面貌日新月异，配套设施不断完善，人文氛围愈发浓厚，巨变中的厦门，未来将释放更加夺目的光彩。

Rural Vitalization

In Xiamen, the sky is blue, the land is green, the water is clean and the people are rich.

Within or outside the island, there are fishing villages and fields. Several beautiful houses are hidden in the green trees. Clean roads surround the village, and a piece of evergreen field is planted in front of or behind the house.

In 2018, a new voice was spread from the rural work conference of Xiamen Municipal Committee: make agriculture a promising industry, make farmer an attractive career and make the countryside a beautiful home to live and work in contentment. Xiamen embarked on a journey of comprehensively deepening rural reforms and fully implementing the strategy of rural vitalization. Today, an excellent transcript for the rural vitalization in Xiamen was submitted – many achievements have been obtained regarding urban modern agriculture, modern construction for beautiful village and rural innovative governance, the economic figures of "agriculture, rural areas and farmers" are constantly being refreshed, and people's income has been raised to a new level.

Here, the villages are beautiful, the environ–ment is clean, the life is happy and the society is harmonious. This is the terraced tea garden located at the military village at the junction of Xiamen, Zhangzhou and Quanzhou. This is the pitaya of Dazhai village and that is the chrysanthemum field of Qiange village. Towards the beautiful blueprint of "prosperous industry, livable ecology, civilized local customs, effective governance, affluent life", the dream of rural vitalization is gradually becoming true.

The villages become prettier and the city becomes newer. The developing Egret Island blows the horn of construction in all small towns and cities. Many new cities are planned to be built. Many new roads are explored and many livelihood projects are established. The construction of the new city opens a window for villagers to look into the world. The appearance of the city keeps changing, and the facilities are also constantly being improved. The humanistic culture atmosphere is becoming stronger. Xiamen, after the huge transformation, will become shinier in the future.

2 乐学
Enjoy Learning

厦门大学

　　山海相伴，风光秀丽，推窗可见落日熔金的海面，她是中国最美的大学之一。1921年，厦门大学由著名爱国华侨领袖陈嘉庚先生创办，成为中国近代教育史上第一所华侨创办的大学。

　　"自强不息，止于至善"，是她的校训。鲜明的办学特色，雄厚的师资力量，使她成为学科门类齐全、国内一流、国际影响广泛的综合性大学，也是国家"211工程"和"985工程"重点建设的高水平大学。

　　近百年来，她培养了40多万名本科生和研究生，成为各个领域的佼佼者，在厦大学习、工作过的两院院士达60多人。

　　厦大深入开展对外交流与合作，与境外240多所高校签署了校际合作协议，与近50所世界排名前200名的高校开展实质性交流合作。与北美洲、欧洲、亚洲、非洲等地区的大学合作建立了15所孔子学院，并获批建设"孔子学院院长学院"。2016年2月，我国第一个在海外建设独立校园的厦大马来西亚分校迎来了首批新生。

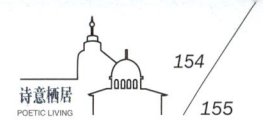

Xiamen University

Xiamen University is surrounded by sea and mountains, which has beautiful scenery. Looking outside the window from the dormitory, you can see the golden sea. It is the most beautiful university in China. In 1921, Xiamen University was founded by Chen Jiageng (Tan Kah Kee), the famous leader of patriotic overseas Chinese. It was the first university founded by overseas Chinese in modern Chinese education history.

"Pursue Excellence, Strive for Perfection" is the school motto of Xiamen University. Distinctive characteristics of education and a strong faculty make it become the first-class influential and comprehensive university with complete categories of disciplines. It is a high-level university that belongs to the national "211 Project" and the "985 Project".

For hundreds of years, the university has cultivated more than 400 thousand undergraduates and post graduates, who later become the leaders in various industries. There are more than 60 academicians of the Chinese Academy of Sciences and Chinese Academy of Engineering who have once studied or worked in Xiamen University.

Xiamen University have also developed its foreign exchanges and cooperation, signing cooperation agreements with more than 240 universities in foreign countries. It also has practical exchanges and collaboration with nearly 50 universities which rank the top 200 in the world. Together with universities in North America, Europe, Asia and Africa, Xiamen University has established 15 Confucius Institutes, becoming the "Dean College of Confucius Institute". On February, 2016, the Malaysia Campus of Xiamen University, China's first overseas independent campus, welcomed the first group of students.

集美学校

　　书香久远，温文尔雅，集美学校是钟灵毓秀之地。著名爱国华侨领袖陈嘉庚先生于1913年倾资创办，是集美各类学校及各种文化机构的总称，享誉海内外。

　　这是融中西风格于一炉的建筑，体现了典型闽南侨乡风格。集美学校包括福南大会堂、图书馆、体育馆、音乐厅、龙舟池、航海俱乐部等设施。

　　学校总建筑面积达3000余亩，拥有在校师生10余万人，形成了由学前教育至小学初中高中、从本科教育到硕士博士教育的人才培养体系。

　　如今，厦门水产学院、集美航海学院、集美师范专科学校、福建体育学院、集美财经专科学校全部并入集美大学，此外，集美学校还包括集美归国侨学生补习学校（华侨大学华文学院）、中国语言文化学校、集美中学、集美小学、集美幼儿园等学校。

Jimei School

The fragrance of book lasts long and people in Jimei School are gentle. It is a place endowed with the fine spirits of the universe. Jimei School was founded in 1913 by Chen Jiageng, the famous leader of patriotic overseas Chinese. It is the general name of all kinds of schools and cultural institutions of Jimei, which is quite famous all around the world.

This is the architecture that combines the features of both Chinese and western buildings, demonstrating the typical building style of southern Fujian. In Jimei School, there are many facilities, such as Funan Town Hall, library, gymnasium, concert hall, dragon boat pond, sailing club and so on.

The area of the school is up to more than 3000 mu (a unit of area). With the total number of more than 100 thousand teachers and students, the school forms a talents cultivation system which includes pre-school education to primary school and junior high school, from undergraduate education to master's degree education.

Today, Xiamen Fisheries College, Jimei Maritime College, Jimei Teachers' College, Fujian Institute of Physical Education, Jimei College of Finance and Economics all integrate into Jimei University. In addition, Jimei School also includes Jimei Tutoring School for overseas students who return to the country (the Chinese Language and Culture College of Huaqiao University), Chinese Language and Culture School, Jimei Middle School, Jimei Primary School, Jimei Kindergarten and other schools.

厦门理工学院

1981年，挟改革开放之风气而创立的厦门理工学院，傲立于中国东南海滨城市厦门，是福建省属公立本科大学，福建省重点建设高校。她的前身鹭江职业大学，是福建省最早的全日制职业技术大学。2003年筹建升本并试招7个专业的本科生，2004年经教育部批准升本并更名为"厦门理工学院"，是133所教育部第二批"卓越工程师教育培养计划"高校之一，国家首批"服务国家特殊需求专业硕士学位研究生教育试点高校"。2013年1月，福建省人民政府批准为"省重点建设高校"。

如今，厦门理工学院有集美、思明、厦软（厦门软件学院）3个校区，全日制在校生20000余人（含研究生、留学生）。学校基本形成学习、研究、实习、产业的学科格局。

Xiamen University of Technology

In 1981, with the trend of reform and opening-up, Xiamen University of Technology was established in Xiamen, a coastal city in the southeast China. It is a public undergraduate university and key university in Fujian province. Its predecessor was Lujiang Vocational University, the earliest full-time vocational university in Fujian province. In 2003, it was planned to be improved to undergraduate school and recruited undergraduates of 7 majors. In 2004, it was approved by the Ministry of Education to be an undergraduate university and changed its name into "Xiamen University of Technology", which was one of the 133 second higher institutions admitted into the "Excellent Engineer Education and Training Program" by the Ministry of Education. It is also among the first batch of "national master's degree graduate education pilot colleges and universities which cultivate professionals for special needs". In January 2013, it was approved by the Fujian municipal government as the "key university of provincial construction".

Today, Xiamen University of Technology has three campuses, namely Jimei, Siming and Xiaruan (Xiamen Software Institute). The number of full-time students in school is more than 20,000 (including graduate students and overseas students). The university has basically formed a discipline pattern of learning, researching, internship and industry.

华侨大学

她是 1960 年在周恩来总理直接关怀下创办的中央部属高校，直属国务院侨务办公室。

华侨大学总部位于著名侨乡泉州，在厦门、泉州形成一校两地的办学格局；现有 28 个教育学院，41 个省部级以上重点学科，94 个本科专业，形成了理工结合、文理渗透、工管相济、协调发展的学科体系。作为国务院侨办华文教育基地和教育部批准的"支持周边国家汉语教学重点院校"，华侨大学创办了"外国政府官员中文学习班"和"安哥拉政府科技人才班"等一系列华文教育品牌项目。

华侨大学是国家重点建设大学、福建省重点建设高校、福建省高水平大学，入选国家特色重点学科项目、"外专千人计划"、"1+2+1中美人才培养计划"创新人才培养实验基地，是福建省继厦门大学之后第二所设有研究生院并具有教授、副教授评审权的高等学府，是新中国最早实行董事会制度的大学。

Huaqiao University

Huaqiao University belongs directly to the central government, established under the care of Premier Zhou Enlai in 1960. It is directly under the State Council Overseas Chinese Affairs Office.

The headquarters of Huaqiao University is located in Quanzhou, a famous hometown of overseas Chinese. It has formed a school-running pattern of one university in two places of Xiamen and Quanzhou. There are 28 educational colleges, 41 provincial and ministerial-level key disciplines and 94 undergraduate majors, forming a discipline system with combination of science and engineering, infiltration of arts and science, mutual benefit of engineering and management and coordinated development. As the Chinese Language and Culture Education Base of the Overseas Chinese Affairs Office of the State Council and a "Key College to Support Chinese Language Teaching in Neighboring Countries" approved by the Ministry of Education, Huaqiao University has established a series of Chinese language education brand projects such as "Chinese Language Learning Class for Foreign Government Officials" and "Angolan Government Science and Technology Talent Class".

Huaqiao University is a national key construction university, a key university in Fujian Province, and a high-level university in Fujian Province. It has been selected into national key disciplines projects, the Recruitment Program of Foreign Experts, "1+2+1 training program of Chinese and American talents", and the innovative talent training experimental base. Following Xiamen University, it is the second higher institution that has graduate colleges and the assessment right of professors and associate professors. It is also the first university in the People's Republic of China to implement the system of board of directors.

厦门一中

厦门一中创办于 1906 年，其前身是清朝康熙二十四年（1685 年）创立的玉屏书院，是厦门岛内最早的书院，厦门的文脉之源。

她英才辈出，享誉中外。涌现了一大批政治家、科学家、教育家、体育明星等。

"勤、毅、诚、敏"，是她的校训；"全省顶尖，全国一流，面向国际，面向未来的现代学校"，是她的办学目标；她以"人文、创新，为发展而教育"为办学理念，坚持培养"国家认同＋国际理解＋人文底蕴＋科学精神"的人才。

她积极履行社会责任，先后创办集美分校等 6 所学校，推进了基础教育均衡发展。

Xiamen No.1 Middle School

Built in 1906, the predecessor of Xiamen No.1 Middle School was the Yuping Academy, which was founded in the 24th year of the Kangxi of the Qing Dynasty (1685). It was the earliest academy within Xiamen Island, and was the cultural origin of Xiamen.

It has cultivated many talents who are well-known both at home and abroad, including a number of politicians, scientists, educators, and sports stars.

The school motto is "diligence, perseverance, integrity and smartness". The education goal is to establish a modern school that is "first class in the province and the country, facing the international and facing the future". The teaching principle is "humanities, innovation and education for development". It also sticks to cultivating talents that "are recognized by the nation, understood by the international community and have cultural knowledge and science spirits".

The school has actively shouldered its social responsibility and set up 6 branch schools including the Jimei branch school. It has promoted the balanced development of preliminary education.

厦门双十中学

1919年，为纪念辛亥革命，厦门霞溪仔街诞生"双十"中学。国学家贺仙舫为学校撰写校歌《勤毅信诚》，选作校训。

她是福建省首批省重点中学之一，在海内外具有较大的影响力。

目前，双十中学拥有枋湖、镇海两个校区。总面积17万平方米、108个班级、5000多名学生。

学校还与台湾台中市双十中学、英国苏格兰博尼斯学院、英国 Westbourne House Prep. School、美国巴尔的摩理工高中、新西兰惠灵顿中学和惠灵顿女子中学多所国外学校结成友好校或姊妹校，长期坚持互访交流。

Xiamen Shuangshi Middle School of Fujian

In 1919, in order to memorize the Revolution of 1911, "Shuangshi (Double Ten)" middle school was established on the Xiaxizai street in Xiamen. He Xianfang, the scholar who studied Chinese ancient civilization wrote it a school song named *Diligence, Perseverance, Trust and Honesty*, which was also the school motto.

It is one of the key middle schools in Fujian province, which has a great influence both at home and abroad.

Currently, Shuangshi middle school has two campuses in Fanghu and Zhenhai, with total area of 170 thousand square meters, 108 classes and over 5,000 students.

This school has cooperated and built up friendships with many other schools both at home and abroad, such as Shuangshi Middle School in Taizhong city of Taiwan, Scotland Bowness College, Westbourne House Prep. School in the UK, Baltimore High School in America, New Zealand Wellington Middle School and Wellington Girls' School.

厦门外国语学校

　　1981年，伴随着厦门经济特区的成立，"海上花园"鼓浪屿诞生了厦门外国语学校。

　　1994年，该校扩大办学规模，迁址到湖滨北路。2004年，又率先把高中部办到海沧，是福建省一级达标中学，福建省重点中学。

　　目前，该校有83个教学班，4500多名学生，360多名教职工。学校共占地10.3万平方米，建筑面积9.32万平方米。

　　厦门外国语学校获得福建省教育厅、省政府对外办公室、省公安厅联合授权，享有接受外国学生资格，是厦门岛内唯一获此资格的中学。她输送了大批优秀生、在校生出国留学，足迹遍及英国、美国、澳大利亚、新加坡等十几个国家，还与日本、法国、加拿大、美国等国家签署了合作办学协议，进行双向交流。

Xiamen Foreign Language School

In 1981, with the establishment of Xiamen Special Economic Zone, Xiamen Foreign Language School was built on Gulangyu Island, the "garden on the sea".

In 1994, the school expanded its educational scale and moved to Hubin North Road. In 2004, it moved its high school to Haicang District. It is the first-level standard middle school and key middle school in Fujian province.

Currently, it has 83 teaching classes, with over 4,500 students and more than 360 staff. The school covers an area of 103,000 square meters, and a construction area of 93,200 square meters.

Xiamen Foreign Language School is authorized jointly by the Education Department of Fujian Province, Foreign Affairs Offiice of the Fujian Provincial People's Government, and the Public Security Bureau in Fujian province. It has the qualification to accept foreign students, and is the only school that has this qualification within Xiamen Island. The school has cultivated many excellent students, and sent many students to study abroad in foreign countries, such as England, America, Australia and Singapore. It has also signed cooperation teaching agreements with several countries such as Japan, France, Canada and America to exchange bilaterally.

3 流韵 Charm

闽南大戏院

　　银白色三角镂空外墙下，映衬着活跃的红，半开放式的玻璃幕墙，增强了剧场的采光效果及建筑空间感。坐落在厦门会展中心北片区的闽南大戏院，外形独特彰显浓郁的海派特色及闽南韵味。

　　总建筑2.78万平方米，她是全省功能最全、规模最大、档次最高、具有国际一流水准的综合性演出场所；她是厦门公共文化设施的新地标，带动厦门"东部文化圈"的形成发展。

　　大剧场金色大厅内"鞋盒式"布局，可容纳1500名观众。采用国际通行的品字形设计的主舞台，舞台机械、灯光、音响设备国内一流。常年举行国内外高水准的大型歌剧、舞剧、综艺晚会，交响乐、室内乐、合唱等演出不断。

Banlam Grand Theater

　　The grand theatre is built by silver white triangle hollow wall, which reflects the dynamic red in the sunshine. The semi-open glass curtain wall enhances lighting effect in the theater and the sense of space in the architecture. Located at the northern part of the Xiamen exhibition center, Banlam Grand Theater has a unique appearance which has a strong foreign style and the charm of South Fujian.

　　With a total construction area of 27,800 square meters, the theatre is the largest comprehensive performance place which has comprehensive functions, and the highest level, world-class standard facilities. It is the new landmark of public culture facilities in Xiamen, enhancing the development of the "eastern culture circle" of Xiamen.

　　The layout inside the golden large hall in the theatre is like a "shoe box", which can contain 1,500 audiences. It adopts the international design of the main stage like the Chinese character " 品 ". The stage machinery, lighting and audio equipment are all first-class in China. It often hosts performances of a high level both at home and abroad every year, including opera, ballet, evening party, symphony, chamber music, and chorus.

海峡大剧院

　　海峡大剧院坐落在厦门岛东海岸的会展片区，与金门岛隔海相望。作为中国金鸡百花电影节第 28 届及未来十年的颁奖场馆，颇受社会各界关注。海峡大剧院总建筑面积 92000 平米，由厦门国际会展中心四期 B8B9 馆及配套东广场地下室组成。

　　B8B9 馆建筑面积 45000 平方米，为单层（局部 2-4 层）30 米高的钢结构建筑，满足各种会议展览兼具剧场演艺功能的综合性建筑；场馆内有一个长 133 米、宽 72 米、高 24 米的主展厅，面积近 10000 平方米，可布置 6920 张座椅，满足电影节颁奖典礼的要求。场馆外观与周边建筑有机协调，在延续原会展片区风格的基础上，采用闽南屋顶挑檐的设计手法，加上四周高耸的柱廊，简洁、通透，独具特色而不失庄重。内部装饰充分融入闽南传统建筑的窗花、红砖元素，顶棚缀满特制的三角梅灯饰，如同爽朗夜空中的星星，寓意着电影节群星璀璨、熠熠生辉。

Strait Grand Theater

Xiamen Strait Grand Theater is located in the Exhibition Area on the east coast of Xiamen Island, facing Kinmen Island across the sea. As the prize-awarding venue of the 28th China Golden Rooster & Hundred Flowers Film Festival and for the next decade, it has attracted a great attention from all sectors of the society. With a total floor area of 92,000 square meters, the Strait Grand Theater is composed of Hall B8B9 of Xiamen International Conference & Exhibition Center Phase IV and the basement of supporting East Square.

The floor area of Hall B8B9 is 45,000 square meters, which is a single-story (2-4-storey in some part) 30-meter-high steel structure construction, meeting the requirements of comprehensive building of various conferences and exhibitions as well as theater performance functions. There is a 133-meter-long, 72-meter-wide and 24-meter-high main exhibition hall inside the construction, providing an area of nearly 10,000 square meters, which can accommodate 6,920 seats, meeting the needs of the award ceremony of the film festival. The outer appearance of the hall is organically coordinated with the surrounding buildings. On the premise of not compromising the continuation of the original style of the Exhibition Area, the hall was designed with an overhanging eaves roof of Southern Fujian flavor and combined with the surrounding majestic colonnade, making it simple, open, unique and solemn. The interior decoration fully integrates the window grille and red brick elements of traditional buildings in Southern Fujian, and the ceiling is decorated with special bougainvillea-shaped lights, just like the stars in the translucent night sky, symbolizing the sparkling stars in the film festival are bright and shining.

嘉庚剧院

　　嘉庚剧院是厦门的一张文化名片，既有与艺术家零距离接触的"市民音乐会"，又有专门面向青少年公益活动的"打开艺术之门"。

　　剧院每年推出多场"市民音乐会"，以各种形式的公益演出、展览、名师讲座等，让市民与吕思清、张海鸥、孙嘉言、潘达等艺术家分享艺术心得，为广大市民带来一场场"音乐交流盛宴"。两获格莱美奖的艺术家埃里奥·瓦多皮安，也携他的"自由星球电台"乐队前来，与厦门观众近距离互动。

　　除了邀请大师授课，剧院还根据不同的演出项目，开展主创见面会、阅读分享沙龙、艺术进校园等活动，培养市民的艺术素养。

Tan Kah Kee (Chen Jiageng) Theater

　　Tan Kah Kee Theater is a cultural name card of Xiamen. It has both "Citizen's Concert" that is in close contact with the artists and "Open the Door of Art" which is a public welfare activity oriented towards the teenagers.

　　The theater launches a number of "Citizen's Concert" every year. In the various forms of public welfare performances, exhibitions and famous teacher lectures, the citizens share their artistic ideas with artists such as Lu Siqing, Zhang Hai'ou, Sun Jiayan and Pan Da, bringing a number of "Music Exchange Feast" to the public. The artist Eliot Wadopian who has won the Grammy Awards twice also brought his "Free Planet Radio" band to interact closely with Xiamen audience.

　　In addition to inviting the masters to teach, the theater also carries out activities such as production team meet-and-greet, reading and sharing salon and introducing the art to the campus based on different performance projects to cultivate the artistic quality of the citizens.

小白鹭艺术中心

白鹭翱翔，是鹭岛厦门的标志性景观。厦门市小白鹭民间舞团，是我国第一个专业民间舞艺术表演团体。她的前身是厦门经济特区与北京舞蹈学院合作创办的北京舞蹈学院中国民间舞专业厦门实验班。

小白鹭艺术中心（金荣剧场），位于厦门岛南端，濒临美丽的厦门湾，美丽的环岛路就在剧院门前，绿树婆娑，轻风细浪，环境优美。

剧场用地1.28万平方米，是厦门市唯一拥有24米深度和多种升降功能的高品位、高规格、多功能的现代化专业舞台的剧场，是厦门艺术学校和厦门小白鹭民间舞团集教研、创作、表演、培训和交流为一体的创作演出场地，又是接待外部演出，满足旅游定点演出的场所。

Xiaobailu Arts Center

The flying egret is the symbol of Xiamen Island. Xiaobailu Civil Dancing Troupe of Xiamen is the first professional folk dancing troupe in China. Its predecessor is the Xiamen experimental class of Chinese folk dancing major in Beijing Dancing Academy, which is co-established by Xiamen Special Economic Zone and Beijing Dancing Academy.

Xiaobailu Art Center (Jinrong Theater) is located the southern end of Xiamen Island, next to the beautiful Xiamen Bay. The beautiful Island Ring Blvd is in front of the theatre. Around the theatre, there are many green trees with gentle wind breezing, forming a good environment.

Covering an area of 12800 square meters, the theater is the only high-taste, high-level and multifunctional modernized professional theater with 24 meters in depth and various functions of rise and fall. It is the performance place for Xiamen Art School and Xiamen Xiaobailu civil dancing troupe to study and research, create, perform, train and communicate with each other. In addition, it is used to receive foreign performance and meet the demands of playing on certain spots.

鼓浪屿音乐厅

　　如果说音乐是鼓浪屿的诗，那么晃岩路1号的鼓浪屿音乐厅就是琴岛鼓浪屿悠远的词牌。世上无限抚琴手，一片乐声在琴岛。在这个诗意栖居的岛上，音乐是通用的交流方式，没有国界的差异，没有沟通的障碍，浓厚的音乐氛围是歌者雅士神往的天堂。

　　1987年，鼓浪屿音乐厅建成并投入使用，其建筑风格独特，环境优雅。数十年来，音乐厅以其独特的建筑风韵和一流的设备设施，先后接待过来自美国、俄罗斯、克罗地亚等多个国家的艺术团体及香港、上海等国内各大乐团的演出，为演出团体、音乐家们及广大观众提供了一系列音乐盛宴。在这座音乐之岛上，鼓浪屿音乐厅是厦门市接待高雅严肃音乐演出的重要场所之一。

Gulangyu Concert Hall

　　If music is the poetry of Gulangyu Island, then Gulangyu Concert Hall at No.1 Huangyan Road is the flagship venue of Gulangyu, the "Piano Island". There are numerous pianists in the world, and the sound of the piano surrounds the Piano Island. Living in this poetic island, music is a universal form of communication without national boundaries or barriers to understanding; with a strong music atmosphere, it is the paradise that singers desire.

　　In 1987, Gulangyu Concert Hall was completed and put into use with a unique architectural style and elegant environment. Over the decades, with its unique architectural charm and leading facilities, the concert hall has hosted performances by art groups from many countries including the United States, Russia and Croatia, and many domestic bands from Hong Kong, Shanghai and other places, providing a diverse musical feast for the performers, musicians and audience members alike. In this island of music, Gulangyu Concert Hall is one of the most important places in Xiamen for the staging of elegant and serious music performances.

4 博物 Museums

厦门市博物馆

博物馆，典藏人类文明的殿堂。厦门市博物馆原在鼓浪屿上的八卦楼，2007年迁至厦门文化艺术中心。新馆包括厦门历史陈列、闽台古石雕大观、闽台民俗陈列和馆藏文物精品展等。

她由厦门博物馆主馆、郑成功纪念馆、厦门经济特区纪念馆、厦门市文化遗产保护中心、思明破狱斗争陈列馆、陈化成纪念馆、陈胜元故居七部分组成，是一座地方综合性博物馆。

厦门市博物馆致力于闽台两岸及传世珍贵文物的收藏、保护、研究、陈列，是我国对外文化交流的重要场所和爱国主义教育的重要基地。

Xiamen Museum

Museum is the palace which stores the human civilization. The original place of Xiamen Museum was at the Eight Diagrams Tower on the Gulangyu Island. In 2007, it moved to Xiamen Cultural and Art Center. The new museum includes Xiamen historical display, Fujian and Taiwan ancient stone statue, Fujian and Taiwan folk art exhibition and collection of cultural relics exhibition.

It consists of seven parts, including the main hall of Xiamen Museum, Zheng Chenggong Memorial Museum, Xiamen Special Economic Zone Memorial Hall, Cultural Heritage Protection Center of Xiamen, Siming Breaking the Prison Struggle Museum, Chen Huacheng Memorial Museum and Chen Shengyuan Former Residence. It is a comprehensive regional museum.

Xiamen Museum is dedicated to the collection, protection, research and display of precious cultural relics which are handed down from ancient times in Fujian and Taiwan. It is an important place for foreign cultural exchanges and patriotism education.

厦门经济特区纪念馆

为纪念改革开放三十周年和厦门经济特区建设二十七周年，在厦门最早的经济特区湖里区，设立厦门经济特区纪念馆。"把经济特区办得更快些更好些"，是邓小平的题词。

厦门经济特区纪念馆占地5000平方米，共四层，分别为厦门经济特区开创阶段、发展阶段、增创新优势和新跨越阶段等四个展馆。

一幅幅风云激荡的照片，记录着厦台交流的每一令人欣喜的瞬间，让人体会到厦门人敢为人先、敢拼敢闯的精神，也仿佛回到那个激动人心的历史时刻。她就像一座历史丰碑，铭刻过去，昭示未来，穿越时光隧道，重温一座滨海小城发展成为海峡西岸重要中心城市的历史进程。

Xiamen Special Economic Zone Memorial Hall

In order to commemorate the 30th anniversary of Reform and Opening Up and the 27th anniversary of the construction of Xiamen Special Economic Zone, Xiamen Special Economic Zone Memorial Hall was established in Huli district, the earliest Special Economic Zone in Xiamen. "Making this Special Economic Zone develop faster and better" is the dedication by Deng Xiaoping.

Covering a total area of 5,000 square meters, Xiamen Special Economic Zone Memorial Hall has four floors, with four exhibition halls respectively representing the beginning stage, developing stage, innovative and advantageous stage and the new breakthrough stage of Xiamen Special Economic Zone.

There are many historical pictures, recording every happy moment of exchanges between Xiamen and Taiwan, which demonstrate the pioneering and enterprising spirit of Xiamen people. They will also bring people back to that exciting historical moment. The museum is like a historic monument, telling the past and looking forward to the future. It goes through the time tunnel to review the historic process of this small coastal city, which has become an important center city on the west side of the strait.

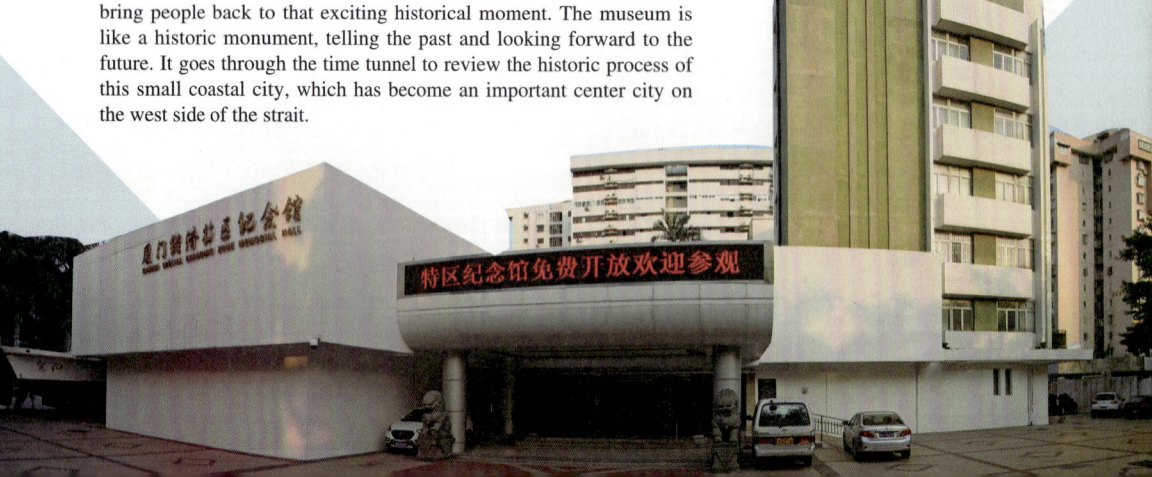

厦门华侨博物院

她是以华侨华人历史为主题的综合性博物馆,是集文物收藏、陈列展览、学术研究为一体的文化教育机构,是福建省和厦门市爱国主义教育基地,也是中国唯一的侨办博物馆。

位于蜂巢山西侧的厦门华侨博物院,是爱国华侨领袖陈嘉庚于1956年9月倡办的。洁白花岗石砌成的宫殿式大楼大门上,镶嵌着廖承志题写的匾额,著名的英籍女作家韩素英赞誉其为"世界上独一无二的华侨历史博物馆",陈嘉庚亲自撰写《倡办华侨博物院缘起》。

博物院设有3个陈列室,分别为华侨历史简介馆、祖国历史文物陈列馆以及自然博物馆,陈列着华侨赠送的礼品,历代货币、青铜器、陶器和雕刻,千余件海内外的鸟兽、水产标本等。

Xiamen Overseas Chinese Museum

It is a comprehensive museum that takes the history of overseas Chinese as the theme. It is the culture and education institution that combines the collection of cultural relics, exhibition, and academic researchs. As the patriotism education base in Fujian province and Xiamen city, the museum is also the only museum that built by overseas Chinese.

Located at the west side of Fengchao Mountain, Xiamen Overseas Chinese Museum was founded in September 1956 by Cheng Jiageng, the leader of patriotic overseas Chinese. The door of this palace-like museum is made up of white granite and hangs a horizontal inscribed board written by Liao Chengzhi. Han Suying, the famous British female writer appraised it as the "unique overseas Chinese history museum in the world". Chen Jiageng also wrote *The Reason of Initiating Overseas Chinese Museum* for it.

There are three display halls in the museum, respectively known as Brief Introduction Hall of Overseas Chinese History, the Exhibition Hall of National Historical Relics, and the Natural Museum. There are displays of presents given by overseas Chinese, ancient currency, bronze, pottery and sculpture, as well as thousands of specimens of animals and birds at home and abroad and aquatic specimens.

陈嘉庚纪念馆

　　陈嘉庚纪念馆，位于嘉庚公园北门以东，是一座社会历史类名人纪念馆。其建筑秉承闽南独特建筑风格，与集美鳌园、嘉庚公园连成一体，交相辉映，构成了一个美轮美奂的旅游纪念地。

　　馆内分为四个展厅，第一至三展厅陈列《华侨旗帜民族光辉——陈嘉庚生平陈列》，展出350多张照片、310多件文物，形象生动地展现了陈嘉庚伟大光辉的一生；第四展厅则展出《在陈嘉庚身边——嘉庚现象诚毅同行》。

　　作为陈嘉庚先生的文物资料收藏馆，陈嘉庚纪念馆充分发挥博物馆的社会教育功能和作用，纪念并发扬嘉庚精神，是厦门重要的爱国主义教育基地。

Tan Kah Kee (Chen Jiageng) Memorial Museum

　　Located at the east of the northern door of Jiageng Park, Tan Kah Kee Memorial Museum is a museum to memorize social and historic celebrities. Its building inherites the unique southern Fujian features, which integrates with Jimei Aoyuan Park and Jiageng Park, forming a magnificent tourist destination.

　　There are four exhibition halls within the museum. From the first one to the third one, *The national glory of Overseas Chinese flag: Chen Jiageng's life* is displayed here, including over 350 photos and 310 cultural relics. It vividly shows the glorious life of Cheng Jiageng. The fourth hall displays *At the side of Chen Jiageng: the real phenomenon of Jiageng*.

　　As the museum that collects the cultural materials of Chen Jiageng, this museum fully exerts the function of social education. It commemorates and promotes the spirit of Jiageng, and is an important patriotic education base in Xiamen.

鼓浪屿钢琴博物馆

一世琴缘，毕生乡情。对钢琴艺术的痴和对故乡桑梓的爱，是华侨胡友义此生的两根主弦，两者交织，催生了这座博物馆。

她位于鼓浪屿景区菽庄花园的"听涛轩"，博物馆里陈列了胡友义收藏的100多架古钢琴，有稀世名贵的镏金钢琴、世界最早的四角钢琴、最早最大的立式钢琴、古老的手摇钢琴、百年前的脚踏自动演奏钢琴和八个脚踏的古钢琴等。

鼓浪屿雅称叫琴岛，方圆1.87平方公里有100多个音乐世家，人均钢琴拥有率为全国第一。得天独厚的优雅的人居环境与之相融，造就了鼓浪屿的音乐传统，培养出周淑安、林俊卿、殷承宗、吴天球、许斐星、许斐平、陈佐煌、许兴艾等大批杰出的音乐家，鼓浪屿因此被中国音乐家协会命名为"音乐之岛"。

Gulangyu Piano Museum

The lifelong love for piano generates a whole life nostalgia for the hometown. The passion for piano and the love for hometown are the two major feelings of Hu Youyi, an overseas Chinese. The two feelings led to the construction of this museum.

The museum is located at the "Ting Tao Xuan" (a pavilion where you can hear the sound of wind) in Shuzhuang Garden on Gulangyu Island. It displays more than 100 ancient pianos collected by Hu Youyi, including the rare and precious golden piano, the world's first upright piano, the earliest and largest vertical piano, the old hand piano, pedal automatic-playing piano of a-hundred-year history and the ancient piano with eight feet.

Gulangyu Island has a beautiful name as "Piano Island". With an area of 1.87 square kilometers, it has over 100 musical families, which ranks the first of the possession rate of piano per person. Together with the advantageous and elegant living environment, the musical tradition on Gulangyu Island has been formulated and large numbers of excellent musicians have appeared, such as Zhou Shuan, Ling Junqing, Yin Chengzong, Wu Tianqiu, Xu Feixing, Xu Feiping, Chen Zuohuang, Xu Xingai. Therefore, Gulangyu Island was entitled "The Island of Music" by the Chinese Musician Association.

故宫鼓浪屿外国文物馆

故宫鼓浪屿外国文物馆坐落于厦门鼓浪屿景区，由厦门市政府与北京故宫博物院合作建设，是北京故宫博物院首次在地方设立的主题馆。

这里是救世医院及护士学校旧址，1898年由美籍荷兰人郁约翰创建，是全国重点文物保护单位。馆内分为"文物来源""科技典范""万国瓷风""生活韵致""典雅陈设""异国情调"等六部分，共展出外国文物219件（套），其中包括来自英国、法国、德国、意大利、美国等国家和地区的各类漆器、陶器、瓷器、织物、钟表等展品，具有极高的欣赏价值。故宫馆藏外国文物精品呈现在这极具异域情调的建筑中，一砖一瓦皆是风情，一器一物尽显内涵，明清时期中西文化交流与交往的历史便如此鲜活了起来。

Kulangsu Gallery of Foreign Artefacts from the Palace Museum Collection

Located in Gulangyu Island Scenic Area of Xiamen, Kulangsu Gallery of Foreign Artefacts from the Palace Museum Collection was jointly constructed by the Xiamen Municipal Government and the Palace Museum, which is the first theme museum set up in a local area by the Palace Museum.

This is the former site of the Hope Hospital and the Nurse School. Founded in 1898 by John Otte, an American Dutchman, it is a key cultural relic under national protection. There are six parts of exhibition: "the source of cultural relics", "the paradigm of science and technology", "the porcelain culture of countries", the "life charm", "elegant furnishings", and the "exotic atmosphere". It exhibits 219 sets of foreign cultural relics, including various exhibits such as lacquer ware, pottery, porcelain, textiles, watches from the United Kingdom, France, Germany, Italy, the United States and other countries and regions, which boasts a high aesthetic value. Foreign cultural relics are presented in this very exotic architecture. Every brick has its own style, and each ware has its unique connotation. Thus, it activates the history of cultural exchanges and communication between China and the West in the Ming and Qing Dynasties.

5 开卷 Reading

社区书院

养生课、国学课、英语课……在湖里金山街道金安社区，一半以上的居民没闲着，忙着上社区书院里的各种课程。"重新走进学堂的感觉真是太好了！"这是居民们对家门口的文化乐园的点赞。

社区高楼林立，居民来自五湖四海，相逢不相识。而社区书院的开办，正在打破"都市冷漠症"的困局。它把社区各种资源充分整合，培育出自己的专业授课团队，拓展课程内容、服务人群，为居民提供新的生活方式。

从有趣的课堂汲取文化养料，在社区书院与邻居们相识相知，让"陌邻"变"睦邻"。大家共同学习成长、协商议事、培育了公民公共精神，打造了真正的居民之家。

厦门社区书院模式，正在全市不断复制推广，遍地开花。

Community Academies

In the Jin'an community of Jinshan Sub-district, Huli District, more than half of the residents are busy learning a variety of courses on community academies, such as health courses, courses for studying Chinese ancient civilization and English classes. "It's so nice to go back to school!" This is the praise from the residents to the culture park in the community.

There are many high-rise buildings in the community, with the residents coming from all corners of the country and not knowing each other even if they meet each other. The establishment of community academies is breaking the predicament of "Urban Apathy". Integrating all kinds of resources in the community, they cultivate their own professional teaching teams, and develop courses to serve people, providing new lifestyles for the residents.

In the community academies, the residents can absorb cultural knowledge from the interesting classes, and they can know each other, thus making "strange neighbors" become "good neighbors". They can learn from each other, grow up together and discuss matters, which cultivates the public spirit of the citizens, and creates a real home for the residents.

The model of Xiamen community academies is constantly spreading throughout the whole city.

筼筜书院

筼筜书院，位于厦门白鹭洲公园东区，2009年7月落成，是厦门第一座现代书院。

竹林环水，桃李缤纷，书院坐落在幽幽翠竹湖畔，秉承竹的雅称，承载君子的梦想，弘扬旧学，培养新知。在邃密与深沉的理念沉淀下，"苟日新，日日新，又日新"，书院逐渐成为书香环绕，人文气息浓郁的文化胜地。

今天的筼筜书院蜚声两岸，在国学普及教育、两岸学术交流、国艺传习等诸方面着力尤多。厦门会晤期间的"习普会"，一年三季的"国学经典公益常设班"活动，近六十场的公益"名家讲座""竹林读书会"，相继举办了十一届的海峡两岸国学论坛……为中华文明的传播，筼筜书院一直勤耕不辍。

Yundang Academy of Classical Learning

Completed in July, 2007, Yundang Academy, the first modern college in Xiamen, was located in the east area of Xiamen Bailuzhou Park.

The academy is situated on the lakeside where the bamboo forest is surrounded by the river and peach trees as well as plum trees are here and there. Adhering to the grace of bamboos, and carrying the dream of gentlemen, the academy develops and expands old knowledge, and cultivates new knowledge. Influenced by the profound ideas, everything is developing, and the academy has gradually become a cultural resort with a rich humanistic atmosphere.

Today's Yundang Academy of Classical Learning is well-known in Taiwan and mainland China. It plays an extremely important role in the universal education of classical learning, academic exchanges across the Taiwan Strait, and learning of national arts. "Meeting between President Xi Jinping and President Vladimir V. Putin" during the BRICS Summit in Xiamen, "Permanent Public Welfare Class for Chinese Classics" activity which is held in three quarters of a year, nearly 60 "Expert Talks" and "Bamboo Forest Book Club" for public welfare and the Cross-Strait Sinology Forum which has been consecutively held for 11 sessions...Yundang Academy of Classical Learning has been working hard so as to spread Chinese civilization.

晓风书屋

　　晓风书屋是厦门的文化地标之一，是厦门读书人的接头地点。她在厦门有几家分店，很多人循着地址找了去，留下许多美好的回忆。

　　这里，你不仅能买到想要的书，还能偶遇想见的人。许多知名学者到厦门来，都曾来逛书店。

　　这家书店的特点，就是书的分类合理，每类书的摆放位置基本固定，熟客想找哪方面的书，进店便直奔某处，非常方便。

Xiaofeng Bookstore

　　As one of the cultural landmark in Xiamen, Xiao Feng Bookstore is the place where Xiamen readers meet each other. She has several branches in Xiamen, and many people go there by following the address, leaving many wonderful memories.

　　Here, you can not only buy the books you want, but also meet the people you want to meet. All the famous scholars who came to Xiamen visited this bookstore.

　　The characteristic of this bookstore is that the book is reasonably classified, and each book has basically a fixed position. Therefore, if frequent visitors want to look for a certain book, they can find it easily, which is very convenient.

纸的时代

这里，纸和文字相遇。

纸的时代不仅有满屋子书，也配有让人做手工、阅读、喝咖啡的地方。阅读的座位几乎都靠窗，满满阳光，满室书香，这样的地方不能不爱。

完整阅读，深度思考，是她的信条。按当当网实时价格打折出售，差价用咖啡券还给读者。以网络售价在实体店售书，恐怕也是她的首创。

书店里面，有九米高的书架、移动的梯子、宽阔的落地窗、舒适的阅读桌椅。拆封过的书，可以随意取阅。除了咖啡区、阅读区，还有沙龙区、展览区和包厢。举办一些小范围的签售、互动和分享活动，不时展出一些当代艺术家的作品。纸品区的纸品，都是环保可再生酸性纸，各具特色和功能，周末开展一些手工制作，有专业老师指点，做玫瑰花、纸鹤、书签等。

Time of Paper Bookstore

Here, paper and words meet with each other.

In the Time of Paper Bookstore, there are not only a large number of books in the room, but also places for people to do handwork, read books and drink coffee. Almost all the seats are near the window, and everyone will love such a place, which is full of sunshine, and full of reading atmosphere.

Full reading and deep thinking are her creeds. Prices of the books are discounted at the prices on Dangdang.com, and the price differences are returned to readers in the form of coffee coupons. To sell books in the physical stores with online prices may be her creation.

In the bookstore, there are high shelves of nine meters, moving ladders, wide French windows, comfortable reading desks and chairs. The books that have been already opened are free to read. In addition to the coffee area, and reading zones, there are also salons, exhibition areas and boxes. She will hold some small-ranged signing sessions, interactions and sharing activities, and exhibit some of the works of contemporary artists from time to time. Paper products are all made of environmentally friendly, renewable, and acidic paper, each with its own features and functions. At the weekend, there are some handcrafting activities, where professional teachers will help you make roses, paper cranes and bookmarks.

十点书店

"从十点开始,阅读成长。"

十点书店的诞生,源自国内知名文化类自媒体"十点读书"。2012年发展至今,十点矩阵全网用户已超过5000万,它用文字和声音,陪伴了无数读者的夜晚。2018年11月23日,十点书店在厦门万象城开业,"十点读书"亦从线上走进线下,走入你的生活里。

十点书店是一家书店,却又不止是一家书店。全店以成长为主题,以十点图书和十点课堂为核心业态,配备十点好物、小十点、十点咖啡,并通过触听装置、十点书房实现与人互动连接,与你一同探索生活的更多可能性。

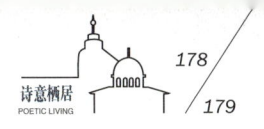

Shidian Reading

"Start at ten o'clock, read and grow."

The birth of Shidian Reading originates from the famed domestic cultural we-media "Read at Ten". Since its development from 2012, Shidian has developed over 50 million matrix network users, using text and sound to keep countless readers company at night. On November 23, 2018, Shidian Reading started business in the MIXC of Xiamen. "Read at Ten" was also developed from online to offline and walked into your life.

Shidian Reading is a bookstore, but it is more than a bookstore. Taking growth as the theme, with Shidian Books and Shidian Class as the core business patterns, equipped with Shidian Goods, Shidian Kids and Shidian Cafe and through touch and audio device and Shidian Sanctum, the bookstore achieves interactive connection with people to explore more possibilities for life with you.

6 风尚 Fashion

万象城

　　万象城位于厦门思明区湖滨南路，是集购物中心、甲级写字楼、精品酒店于一体的都市综合体。作为华润置地入驻福建的首个高端商业作品，万象城力图打造华东南首个"Luxury+"旗舰级消费新地标，引进超过25个国际一线奢侈品品牌，同时规划了近300个精品品牌门店，用"遍寻世间好物"的招商理念，为华东南区域消费者臻选最优产品阵列，设计最佳业态组合。在基础的"衣、食、住、行"以外，万象城还在"知、健、美、爱"方面为消费者提供更全的商品与服务。福建首家华润自营的万象影城、福建首家言几又书店旗舰店都为消费者提供了精神的栖息场所，助力厦门家庭生活品质提升；另外，全球臻选、坚持"发源地引进、一个地方菜只选一家"的餐厅品牌组合，也为本土消费者创造了新鲜的用餐体验。

The Mixc

　　Located in Hubin South Road, Siming District, Xiamen, the Mixc is an urban complex integrating shopping center, grade A office building and boutique hotel. As the first high-end commercial work of CR Land in Fujian, the Mixc is striving to build the first "Luxury+" new landmark of flagship consumption in southeast China, introducing more than 25 international first-line luxury brands while planning to set nearly 300 boutique brand stores, using the investment philosophy of "in searching of good things in the world" to select the best array of products and design the best trade mix for the consumers in southeast China. In addition to the basic "clothing, food, shelter and transportation", the Mixc also provides the consumers with more comprehensive goods and services in the aspect of "knowledge, health, beauty and love". Both the first self-run Mixc Cinema of CR Land in Fujian and the first flagship store of the YanJiYou bookstore in Fujian give the consumers a spiritual habitat and help to promote the life quality of Xiamen families; in addition, the globally selected restaurant brand combinations adhering to "introducing from the original place, and selecting only one restaurant for each local cuisine" also create a fresh dining experience for the local consumers.

中华城

中华城是高端的综合性景观型商业中心，集旅游、购物、餐饮、娱乐、休闲、品读等诸多功能为一体。值得一提的是，中华城是从消费者消费感受的角度构建起来的、符合现代消费者消费理念的商业中心，其努力营造中西合璧的人性化购物环境，致力于提升顾客健康时尚的生活品位。中华城借助中山路核心商圈的引力，营造与国际接轨的大型商业中心，进一步扩大中高端消费市场，扩大厦门中华城在全国的影响力，展现了国内外流行品牌的魅力与风采。

China City

As a high-end integrated landscape business center, China City combines tourism, shopping, catering, entertainment, leisure and reading as one. It is worth mentioning that the China City is a business center built from the perspective of consumers, which conforms to the modern consuming concept of consumers. It is committed to create a humanized shopping environment with both Chinese and Western characteristics, thus improving customer's taste of life in health and fashion. With the help of the central business district of Zhongshan Rd, China City builds a large commercial center with international standards to further expand the high-end consuming market, and to expand the influence of China City in the whole country, which shows the charm and style of popular brands at home and abroad.

磐基中心

　　磐基中心位于厦门思明区嘉禾路，磐基名品中心与磐基希尔顿酒店、磐基的国际甲级商务楼并称为磐基中心的三驾马车，三位一体，共同引导厦门的高端消费。从当季最新的时尚潮流商品，到韵味极致的美食体验，再到格调优雅的购物空间，磐基国际名品中心全方位提供与世界潮流精彩同步的品质生活体验，实现高端购物、餐饮、休闲一体的购物体验。

Paragon Shopping Mall

　　Paragon Shopping Mall is located in Jiahe Rd of Xiamen Siming District, and Paragon International Brand Center (Paragon Shopping Mall) together with Hilton Xiamen and Paragon International Class-A Commercial Building is known as the troika of the paragon center, which guides the high-end consumption in Xiamen. From the latest fashion commodities, to delicious food, to the elegant style of shopping space, Paragon International Brand Center provides a full range of high-quality life experience synchronizing with the world trend, which can finally offer you an integrated shopping experience of high-end shopping, catering, and leisure.

JFC 品尚中心

　　JFC 品尚中心位于厦门会展北片区，环岛路与展鸿路交汇处，为两岸金融中心重点核心发展区，是建发房地产集团在厦门区域的首个商业项目，是福建首家艺术文化购物中心。其高端而独具特色的购物环境辐射岛内外，为厦门带来一种全新的艺术生活方式。JFC 品尚中心毗邻香山游艇会和闽南大戏院，主打中高端消费群体，其环境优美，规模宏大，是休闲娱乐购物的理想去处。

SM 商业城

　　SM 商业城是菲律宾 SM 集团投资中国市场的第一站，位于仙岳路和嘉禾路交界处，SM 城市广场（SM 一期）热闹繁华，SM 新生活广场（SM 二期）时尚高雅，玻璃的人行天桥串联起两大商城，让游人自在地享受穿行购物的乐趣。SM 商业城以其丰富齐全的商品业态，将"一站式"购物、娱乐、美食、体闲的消费生活理念诠释得淋漓尽致，成为厦门市乃至周边地区地标式的消费首选地。SM 集团将在 SM 一期、二期项目北部投建 SM 三期项目，建成后，将集世界品牌店、室内外餐厅、咖啡厅、健身娱乐中心以及高端商务办公楼为一体，成为一个全业态的新兴商业城。

SM City

　　Located in the intersection of Xianyue Rd and Jiahe Rd, SM City is Philippines SM Group's first station of investing in China. SM City Plaza (SM Phase 1) is lively and prosperous while SM New Life Plaza (SM Phase 2) is full of fashion and elegance. The vitreous passenger foot-bridge connects the two big malls, allowing visitors to enjoy the pleasure of shopping. With rich commercial models, SM City shows completely the ideas of consumption and life including "one-stop" shopping, entertainment, delicacy and leisure, becoming the first-choice landmark consuming place in Xiamen city and the surrounding areas. SM Group will build SM Phase 3 project in the north of SM Phase I and SM Phase 2 project. After building the SM Phase 3 project, SM City will combine world brand stores, indoor and outdoor restaurants, coffee shops, fitness and entertainment centers and the high-end business office building as one, thus becoming an emerging commercial city with a full industry.

JFC Pinshang Center

　　Located in the north area of Xiamen conference and exhibition center and the intersection of Island Ring Blvd and Zhanhong Rd, JFC Pinshang Center is the core development area of cross-strait financial center. It is the first commercial project of C&D Real Estate Corporation Limited In Xiamen, and is the first shopping center of art and culture in Fujian. Its high-end and unique shopping environment influences people both inside and outside the island, bringing a new art lifestyle for Xiamen. Adjacent to the Xiangshan yacht club and Banlam Grand Theater, JFC Pinshang Center focuses on the mid-high-end consumers, and has a beautiful environment and a large scale. It is an ideal place for leisure, entertainment and shopping.

湾悦城

湾悦城位于厦门市新客厅——五缘湾高端核心商圈，是厦门建发房地产集团2016年的商业力作，汇聚生活、美食、亲子、名品五大主力业态；集合服饰、珠宝、箱包、家具、餐饮、儿童等近150个国内外知名品牌，凭借独道的高品质、新生活方式主张，勾勒出厦门湾区一个全新的多彩生活空间。

OnePark

OnePark is located in the new "living room" of Xiamen City – Wuyuan Bay high-end core business area. It is a commercial masterpiece of Xiamen C&D Corporation Limited in 2016 which brings together the five major business patterns including living, food, parent-child and brand products and integrates nearly 150 well-known brands in domestic and abroad regarding clothing, jewelry, bags, furniture, catering and kids. With the unique proposition of a high-quality and new lifestyle, it portrays a completely new and colorful living space in the bay area of Xiamen.

宝龙一城

宝龙一城位于厦门市思明区金山路与吕岭路交汇处，作为厦门东部规模体量最大的商业体，宝龙一城首创"六位一体"商业综合体，以购物中心为核心，融汇五星级酒店、超五A甲级写字楼、服务式公寓、SOHO与艺术中心，成为厦门新地标。

Powerlong One Mall

Powerlong One Mall is located at the intersection of Jinshan Road and Lvling Road in Siming District of Xiamen City. As a commercial complex which has the largest scale in the east of Xiamen, Powerlong One Mall created the first commercial complex of "Six in One", with shopping center as the core and five-star hotels, super 5A Grade A office buildings, service apartments, SOHO and art centers integrated, making it a new landmark of Xiamen.

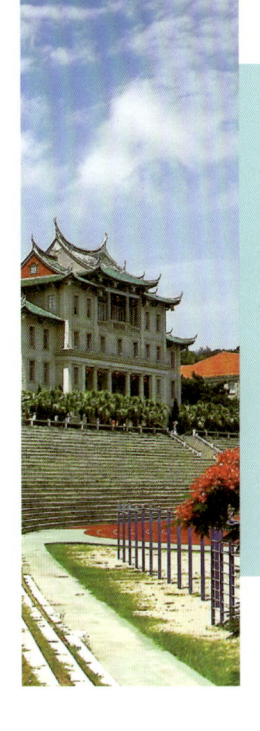

I have gone through every corner of the city,
Not for meeting,
Just to feel your beauty,
And remember your image!

走遍城市的每一个角落，

不为遇见，

只为感受你的美好，

铭刻你的印象！

印象 XIAMEN 厦门

编委会

主　　编:	李辉跃							
副 主 编:	上官军	江曙曜						
执行编辑:	沈　萍							
编　　务:	汪　波	林　君	谢诚伟	詹　文	林　婧	陈科颖	颜艺芬	刘茜茹	谢　坤
	林心韵	杨吟越	庄小梅	蔡丽明					
装帧设计:	厦门华亿内容产业有限公司							
图片支持:	王友学	王火炎	石　灿	朱庆福	朱毅力	李国兴	杨景初	吴　伟	张天骄
	张晓良	陈亚都	陈伟凯	陈轻松	陈健中	林志杰	林铭鸿	林彩凤	林新瑜
	周赞家	赵伟权	赵建军	洪志武	洪蔚尼	姚毅文	徐金跃	黄少毅	黄　嵘
	梁　伟	廖　健	潘建鹏	魏克丰					
	(按姓氏笔画排列)								

图书在版编目(CIP)数据

印象厦门:汉英对照/厦门市人民政府新闻办公室编.—厦门:厦门大学出版社,2017.8(2020.6重印)
ISBN 978-7-5615-6540-7

Ⅰ.①印… Ⅱ.①中… Ⅲ.①厦门-概况-汉、英 Ⅳ.①K925.73

中国版本图书馆 CIP 数据核字(2017)第 138833 号

出版人	郑文礼
责任编辑	王鹭鹏　曾妍妍
出版发行	厦门大学出版社
社　　址	厦门市软件园二期望海路 39 号
邮政编码	361008
总编办	0592-2182177　0592-2181406(传真)
营销中心	0592-2184358　0592-2181365
网　　址	http://www.xmupress.com
邮　　箱	xmup@xmupress.com
印　　刷	厦门市竞成印刷有限公司
开本	787mm×1092mm　1/16
印张	12.5
插页	4
字数	241 千字
印数	10 201～14 200 册
版次	2017 年 8 月第 1 版
印次	2020 年 6 月第 2 次印刷
定价	58.00 元

本书如有印装质量问题请直接寄承印厂调换

厦门大学出版社
微信二维码

厦门大学出版社
微博二维码

真像海底一般的奥妙啊，

真像龙宫一般的晶莹，

真像山林一般的幽美啊，

真像仙境一般的明静，

凤凰木开花红了一城，

木棉树开花红了半空，

榕树好似长寿的老翁，

木瓜有如多子的门庭，

鹭江唱歌唱亮了渔火，

南海唱歌唱落了繁星，

五老峰有大海的回响，

日光岩有如鼓的浪声。

——郭小川 《赞厦门》

BEAUTIFUL XIAMEN

真水厦门

Mysterious like the seabed,

Sparkling like the Dragon Palace,

Graceful like the mountain forest,

Bright like the wonderland,

Delonix regia bloom, tinting the whole city.

Bombax blooms, reddening the half sky.

Banyans are like the longevous men.

Papayas are like the large families with many children.

Singing on the Lujiang River is accompanied by the lights on fishing boats.

Singing on the South China Sea is accompanied by an array of stars.

There are echoes of the sea on Wulao Peak.

There is sound of waves like a drum on Sunlight Rock.

- The Praises of Xiamen by Guo Xiaochuan

真水厦门

BEAUTIFUL XIAMEN

真像海底一般的奥秘啊，
真像龙宫一般的晶莹，
真像山林一般别画美啊，
真像仙境一般的明朗。
凤凰木花红了一城，
木棉树开花红了半空。
榕树好似长寿的老翁。
木瓜有如多子的门庭。
鹭江吼歌唱着了渔火，
南海吼歌唱着了繁星。
五老峰有大海的回响。
日光岩有如鼓的涛声。

——郭小川 《赞厦门》

Mysterious like the seabed,
Sparkling like the Dragon Palace,
Graceful like the mountain forest,
Bright like the wonderland,
Delonix regia bloom, tinting the whole city,
Bombax blooms, reddening the half sky,
Banyans are like the longevous men,
Papayas are like the large families with many children,
Singing on the Lujiang River is accompanied by the lights on fishing boats,
Singing on the South China Sea is accompanied by an array of stars,
There are echoes of the sea on Wulao Peak,
There is sound of waves like a drum on Sunlight Rock.

— The Praises of Xiamen by Guo Xiaochuan